Guide to Zimbabwe & Botswana

Guide to Zimbabwe & Botswana

David Else

BRADT PUBLICATIONS

First published in 1994 by Bradt Publications, 41 Nortoft Rd, Chalfont St Peter, Bucks SL9 0LA, England.
Published in the USA by The Globe Pequot Press, 6 Business Park Road, PO Box 833, Old Saybrook, CT 06475-0833.
Distributed in Southern Africa by Media House Publications, PO Box 782395, Sandton 2146, South Africa.

Copyright © 1994 David Else

All rights reserved. No part of this publication may be reproduced, stored in a retrieval system, or transmitted in any form or by any means, electronic, mechanical, photocopying or otherwise without the written consent of the publishers.

British Library Cataloguing in Publication data
A catalogue record of this book is available from the British Library.

ISBN 0 946983 16 X

US Library of Congress Cataloging-in-Publication Data
A catalog record for this book is available from the Library of Congress

US ISBN 1-56440-566-4

Cover photo: Keith Jones (Images of Africa)
Maps, cartoons and drawings by Jill Bitten
Typeset from the author's disc by Patti Taylor, London NW10 1JR
Printed in Great Britain by BPC Wheatons Ltd, Exeter

THANKS

I would like to thank the many people who helped me write this guidebook. It's always difficult to name everybody individually. Those who were involved know who they are and just how much invaluable help they were able to give.

Firstly, many thanks to Chris McIntyre for a good deal of detailed information on Maun and the Okavango. Chris is the author of Bradt Publications' *Guide to Namibia and Botswana*. He has worked in southern Africa for three of the last six years, and is currently researching and writing further, more detailed, guides to the region.

For contributions, to the several editions of this book, I'd like to thank all the readers who wrote with new information, especially Simon Atkins, Martin Gascoigne, Jurgen Lieb, Jacqui Green, Neil Irving, John Doyle, Paul Hunt, David Bellusci, Tom Edwards, Rev Denys Whitehead, Lars Andersson, Michal Bahat, Alfred Kirchof, Robert Jackson, Richard Wood, Margaret Cullum, Tony Chambers, Kate Worster, Diana Clement, Gail Davey, Jenny Mothoneos, Chris and Emma Tatton, Robin Saxby, Flea Snowsill, Michael Cotton, Lesley Allwood-Coppin, Luc Lebeau, Sue Matthews and Tom Woods. Their returned dog-eared copies, complete with margin notes, or letters full of updates, corrections and new insights, were invaluable and very much appreciated.

Thanks also to the people of Zimbabwe and Botswana, and to the travellers from around the world, who willingly (or unknowingly) supplied me with their comments and impressions.

And, of course, special thanks should go to you, the reader, for buying this book! I hope you enjoy Zimbabwe and Botswana as much as I did. Things are always changing, especially in a place like Africa, so if you have any new information, please send it to me at Bradt Publications. The info will be used in the next edition of this book, and your name will appear on this page. I look forward to hearing from you.

D.E., Sheffield, 1994

Contents

PART ONE: ZIMBABWE 1
Chapter One: Facts and figures 3

Chapter Two: Cities and Towns 11
Bulawayo 13, Harare 14, Kariba 18, Masvingo 19, Mutare 20.

Chapter Three: Hiking 25
Matobo National Park 25, The Nyanga Mountains 30, Chimanimani National Park 38, Mavuradonha Wilderness Area 46.

Chapter Four: Places of Interest 49
Bvumba Mountain 49, Chinhoyi Caves 50, Hwange National Park 51, Mana Pools National Park 51, Great Zimbabwe Ruins 52, Victoria Falls 53

PART TWO: BOTSWANA 57
Chapter Five: Facts and Figures 59

Chapter Six: Cities and Towns 63
Gaborone 63, Francistown 65, Ghanzi 65, Kasane 66, Nata 66, Maun 66.

Chapter Seven: The Okavango Delta 67

Chapter Eight: Places of Interest 75
Moremi Wildlife Reserve 75, Chobe National Park 76

PART THREE: GENERAL INFORMATION 77
Chapter Nine: Health and Security 79
Before you go 79, Diseases and how to avoid them 80, Other health tips 83, Security 84.

Chapter Ten: Things to Take 85
In your rucksack 85, In your wallet 88.

Chapter Eleven: Miscellaneous 89

Appendix
Books and maps 91
Index 95

MAPS

Zimbabwe	**2**
Bulawayo	12
Harare	16
Matobo National Park	24
Nyanga National Park	32
Chimanimani National Park	40
Botswana	**58**
Gaborone	64
Maun	68

INTRODUCTION

As its name implies, this book is a concise comprehensive guide to travelling in Zimbabwe and Botswana. It contains all the advice and information that you, the independent overland traveller, need to survive. It may even help you enjoy yourself! It will definitely help you decide where to go and what to do when you get there.

The greatest advantage, however, about this No Frills Guide is the accuracy and relevance of the information it contains. All the information was gathered by travellers who have recently returned from Zimbabwe and Botswana. Constant up-dating is something that more elaborate guidebooks could never do. Although this guide may appear to be basic, the content is bang up to date! You're paying for hard facts, not soft frills.

It's important to remember, though, that all over Africa so many things are changing at such a rate that it's impossible for any book to remain accurate for very long. This book is as reliable as it's possible to be, but please use it as a GUIDE only. Do not rely on it totally. Combine the advice it contains with what you can gather along the way. Your best source of up-to-date information in any country is always other travellers and the local people themselves. Never be afraid to ask; it'll make your travelling easier and much more enjoyable.

If there is anything you do find that we've got wrong, or you think there's something that should be included in our next edition, please write as soon as you can to let us know, then we can keep other travellers informed. Some of the information we have recently received from travellers has been included in its original form; this is printed in italics.

Send it to: Bradt Publications, 41 Nortoft Road, Chalfont St. Peter, Bucks SL9 0LA, England.

ZIMBABWE & BOTSWANA
Okavango Wildlife & Bushmen

A total 'Old Africa' experience. 3 weeks from Harare, travelling by 4WD truck, train and native canoe. Into the remote and uninhabited wilderness of the Okavango Delta, a wildlife haven, meeting the nomadic Ikung bushmen, game viewing in Chobe National Park, and a visit to Victoria Falls, the 'Smoke that Thunders'. Contact us for full details of departure dates and cost. The Explore brochure also includes Zaire, Rwanda, Uganda, Tanzania, Algeria, Morocco, and descriptions of over 50 other tours, treks and expeditions worldwide.

EXPLORE

Explore Worldwide (ZB), 7 High Street, Aldershot, Hants GU11 1BH, UK.   ☎ 0252 319448

'A traveller without knowledge is like a bird without wings.'
Mushariff-Ud-Din (1184-1291)

STANFORDS

The World's Largest Map and Travel Book Shop

AT 12-14 LONG ACRE LONDON WC2E 9LP
MAIL ORDER SERVICE   TEL 071 836 1321 FAX 071 836 0189

AND STANFORDS AT BRITISH AIRWAYS
156 REGENT STREET LONDON W1R 5TA

PART ONE

ZIMBABWE

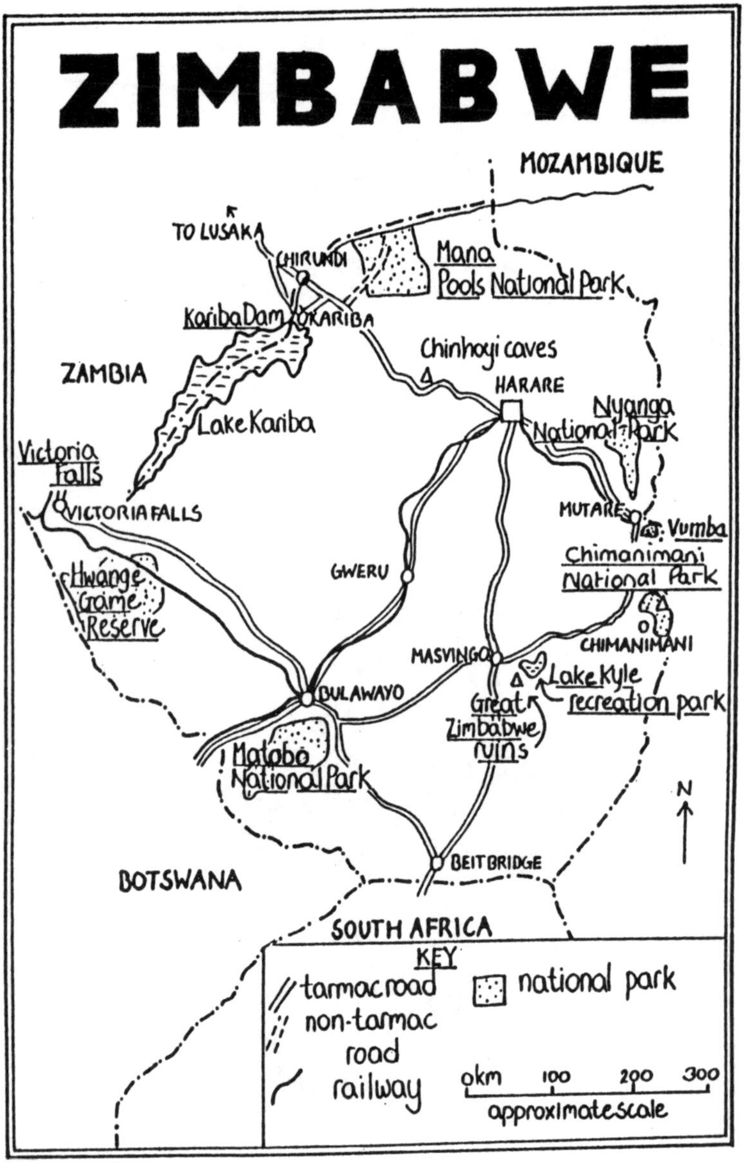
ZIMBABWE
MOZAMBIQUE
TO LUSAKA
CHIRUNDI
Mana Pools National Park
Kariba Dam
KARIBA
Chinhoyi caves
ZAMBIA
HARARE
Nyanga National Park
Lake Kariba
Victoria Falls
VICTORIA FALLS
MUTARE
Vumba
Chimanimani National Park
GWERU
Hwange Game Reserve
CHIMANIMANI
MASVINGO
Lake Kyle recreation park
BULAWAYO
Great Zimbabwe ruins
Matobo National Park
N
BEITBRIDGE
BOTSWANA
SOUTH AFRICA
KEY
tarmac road
national park
non-tarmac road
railway
0km 100 200 300
approximate scale

Chapter One

Facts and figures

Zimbabwe measures 390,000 square kilometres (156,000 sq. miles), about twice the size of England and Scotland, or about half the size of Texas. The central parts of the country (called the High Veld) are mainly over 1,000 metres above sea level, and consist largely of farmland, punctuated by granite outcrops. In the Eastern Highland region, on the border with Mozambique, the land rises to over 2,000 metres. The northern and southern regions are lower, with less rainfall and warmer temperatures.

Zimbabwe's hot season is from October to March, with rain between December and March: temperatures average 27°C, although they can rise above 35°C in low lying areas such as Mana Pools in the Zambezi Valley. The cool season is from April/May to September: temperatures average 15°C, but drop a lot lower in the mountains.

The best time to visit is between May and September. August is the peak of the tourist season, and worth avoiding if you can.

Manufacturing is diversified: Zimbabwe exports tobacco, iron and steel, cotton products and asbestos.

People and languages

In July 1988, the estimated population of Zimbabwe was 10 million. This is expanding rapidly. The two major groups of people ('tribes') are Shona (70%) and Matabele (25%). Most of the African population in rural areas are subsistence farmers or labourers on ranches and plantations. There are less than 100,000 people of European origin in Zimbabwe, involved mainly in farming and commerce.

English is the national language, widely spoken. The two main local languages are Shona and Ndebele (spoken by the Matabele).

Historical points

The first major organised state to become established in this region was based around the city of Great Zimbabwe, where huge stone walls and other remains can still be seen today. This state covered much of modern-day Zimbabwe and parts of Mozambique between the 11th and 15th Centuries, and was at its height of power between 1300 and 1400.

Further north, the Mwena Mutapa state became established as Great Zimbabwe declined. With territory spreading eastwards to the coast, this state traded with Arab and Swahili merchants and later came into contact with Portuguese navigators. By the early 17th Century the Mwene Mutapa state was under Portuguese control.

However, by the end of this century, the Portuguese had been forced back to the coast and another new state, called Rozwi, or Rozvi, became a powerful force in the region.

The Rozwi flourished until early in the 19th century when, further south, in what is now northern South Africa, the Zulu King Shaka expelled one of his generals, Mzilikazi, who led his people north over the Limpopo River to oust the Rozwi and found Matabeleland.

In 1888, Mzihkazi's son Lobengula signed a treaty with the European settlers heading north from South Africa, allowing them to mine gold in Matabeleland. This led to an increase in the number of white settlers, until war broke out in 1893. Lobengula was killed and the whole kingdom came under the control of the British South Africa Company.

In 1923 the region became the separate colony of Southern Rhodesia, a member of the British Empire. Increasing numbers of whites from South Africa and Europe settled in Rhodesia, and conditions under which the blacks lived and worked continued to get worse.

This eventually led to the founding of two political parties: The Zimbabwe African People's Union (ZAPU) and the Zimbabwe African National Union (ZANU). Both parties were banned in the early 1960s after various acts of sabotage were caused by party activists because the Rhodesian Prime Minister, Ian Smith, had refused to agree to any of their demands.

In 1965 Ian Smith issued a Unilateral Declaration of Independence (U.D.I.), cutting all colonial ties with Britain. In response, sanctions were imposed by Britain and some other countries but to no great effect. Meanwhile ZANU and ZAPU stepped up their acts of sabotage, and based in neighbouring countries, began to fight an outright guerilla war. By the mid 1970s the guerillas, especially ZANU

Facts and figures

(who operated out of Mozambique into Eastern Rhodesia), had succeeded in forcing large numbers of whites to leave the country.

Various attempts were made by other African and European countries to end the conflict and work towards a solution bringing together the whites and blacks, and to a lesser extent the two black factions. Eventually full independence was granted in April 1980 with the whites keeping twenty seats in the 100 seat parliament, but all political power going to the black leaders. (The allocation of twenty white seats was abolished in 1987, but whites still play a part in government.)

In the early 1980s, old disagreements between ZANU (mainly supported by members of the Shona tribe) and ZAPU (mainly Matabele) resurfaced, with Joshua Nkomo (the ZAPU leader) accused of plotting against President Robert Mugabe (the leader of ZANU). In 1988 a unity agreement led to Matabele dissidents laying down their arms and, in December 1989, Mr Nkomo and ZAPU were finally integrated into Mr Mugabe's ZANU government.

In March 1990 country-wide elections were held for the post of president and for members of parliament. Mr Mugabe's main opposition came from Mr Edward Tekere, leader of the newly formed Zimbabwe Unity Movement (ZUM). Mr Tekere was formerly a minister in Mr Mugabe's government but was expelled after he launched a campaign against corruption. Mr Mugabe won the presidential election and his party won all but three of the 120 seats available in the general election.

Impressions

Most travellers report that all Zimbabweans are very friendly. Jacqui Green, a traveller from Britain, writes: *As a single woman traveller I never once felt under threat. I soon learned that complete strangers approaching in the street is genuine friendship and nothing more sinister.*

Lesley Allwood-Coppin, also from Britain, wrote to agree with Jacqui: *Zimbabwe is a cosmopolitan country with a warmth and welcome for everyone. I met with nothing but friendship and kindness.*

Lars Andersson, from Sweden, writes: *Beware of over-polite 'students' showing little white papers and asking for contributions.*

In recent years travellers have reported an increasing number of robberies in Harare. You should obviously avoid back streets after dark but, even in the city centre during the day, it seems a few muggings and snatch-thefts have occured. This situation appears to be limited to Harare, but keep your valuables safely hidden wherever you are. In any town, watch out for pickpockets in markets and bus stations.

Coming and going
Air
For travellers going directly to Zimbabwe, there are frequent flights from many European capitals to Harare. London is the cheapest place in Europe to buy flights to southern Africa: check Africa Travel Shop (071-387 1211), African Travel Systems (071-602 5091), STA (071-465 0486) and Trailfinders (071-938 3366) for bargains and special deals on other aspects of travel such as safaris and accommodation.

To get between the airport and Harare centre, the airport bus connects with most international flights, and costs Z$15. Taxis cost around Z$50. If the airport bank is closed, taxi drivers may accept the fare in US dollars (around US$8), although you should be discrete when asking.

Flying out of Harare, all non-residents must pay an airport departure tax of US$20. This should be done at a bank, and can be paid for in any foreign currency. Your air ticket is stamped to show the payment has been made. In emergencies the stamp can be bought at the airport, but this must be in US dollars, and no change is given.

Land
For overland travellers the main border crossing points with Botswana are at Plumtree and Kazungula, and with South Africa at Beitbridge. All land border crossing points are closed at night.

Neil Irving, a traveller from Britain, writes: *On the train crossing at Plumtree, from Zimbabwe into Botswana, we had a four hour wait but no other problems apart from the train running out of drinks! Passengers would dash to a nearby bottle-store, hoping the train would not depart while they were gone!*

It is possible to transit through Mozambique between Harare and Blantyre (Malawi) by hitching a ride with the daily convoy, known as the 'Gun Run', passing through territory alternately held by the Mozambique army and Renamo rebel forces. The situation is notoriously unpredictable and the journey potentially lethal, but during 'quiet periods' many travellers use this route. Check at the Mozambique embassy in Harare or Malawi.

Facts and figures

If you're heading north out of Zimbabwe, towards Tanzania and Kenya, you may be able to get a ride on an overland truck. These carry groups of people from Nairobi down to Victoria Falls or Harare and sometimes return empty, carrying anyone who wants to cross half the continent quickly and cheap. The return trip takes about four days and the 'fare' seems to be negotiable. The trucks can be found parked up at the campsites in Harare and Vic Falls.

Regulations

Citizens of Commonwealth countries, most European countries and the USA do not need entry visas, but do require an onward air ticket and proof of 'sufficient funds'. A Miscellaneous Charges Order (MCO) is not acceptable, but a dated ticket out of another African country should be accepted. 'Sufficient funds' is usually interpreted to mean enough to buy a flight out of the country (if you don't already have a ticket) and to support yourself during your stay. You should check current regulations with your nearest Zimbabwe embassy or tourist office. There are also regulations on the amount of Zimbabwean money you can take in or out of the country, currently Z$100. There is no limit to the amount of foreign currency that can be brought into Zimbabwe.

Money

The Zimbabwe dollar (Z$) is divided into 100 cents (c). The official rate of exchange in 1990 was UK£1 = Z$4, US$1 = Z$2.5, and in 1993 it was UK£1 = Z$9, US$1 = Z$5. In 1994, the official rate of exchange was UK£1 = Z$12, US$1 = Z$8. Visitors should expect similar increases in future years.

However, although inflation is high and prices rise dramatically every year, the exchange rates increase also, so eventual costs to the visitor remain generally the same. In this chapter, prices are quoted in US$ to help you get an idea of costs and budget for a trip. In chapters two, three and four prices are quoted in Z$. Where prices are quoted in Z$ use the rates here to convert them to US$ or UK£. (On the blackmarket it is sometimes possible to get twice as much as the official bank rate, but this is obviously illegal and penalties are high if you're caught.)

Visitors to Zimbabwe will notice that prices for most hotels, organised tours and flights are quoted in US dollars. You can pay directly in US dollars (or another hard currency) by cash or travellers cheques. Most international credit cards are also accepted. Alternatively you can pay in Zimbabwe dollars at the current rate of exchange, but this incurs an extra 10% sales tax. Most travellers agree that for these larger payments US dollars is cheaper and easier.

You should also note that different prices are often applied for foreign visitors and for Zimbabwean citizens. For example, hotel rates for Zimbabweans are about half that for foreigners. However, in tourist 'low' seasons, foreigners can often get hotel rooms or tours at the citizens' rate, or somewhere in between.

Transport

Road Zimbabwe has an extensive network of good quality tarred roads. Express buses run between Harare and other major towns at least once per day in each direction. Services are fast and reliable, and fares are reasonable: around US$7 for Harare to Matere or Bulawayo. Seats can be reserved in advance; often necessary at weekends.

Hitch-hiking is generally quick and easy. You should expect to pay about the same as a local bus fare if you get a lift in a lorry or pick-up van (which is fair, as even the local people have to pay), but drivers with saloon cars usually give lifts for free, and will often go out of their way to help you.

'Local' buses operate between every town and village in the country. These are usually slower and more crowded than express buses, and rarely used by tourists.

Taxis around Harare are good value when the fare is shared by three or four. Meters always work, and are usually reliable, even if everything else in the car is broken. If in doubt check the price before getting in. But be quick, or someone else will take your cab!

'Emergency taxis' (large 7 or 9 seater cars) follow bus routes and carry many passengers on a cost-sharing basis. They're cheaper than ordinary taxis but routes are difficult to work out and queues are long.

Lars Andersson, from Sweden, sent the following advice: *If you go on local buses, bring earplugs. The noise is terrible!*

Rail Zimbabwe National Railways offers services to all major points within the country and connections to stations in neighbouring countries. Trains run between Bulawayo and Harare and between Bulawayo and Victoria Falls; you can also travel between Bulawayo and Mafeking, South Africa (via Francistown, Botswana), and between Harare and Mutare. There are express trains, which travel

Facts and figures 9

at night, and local trains, which are slower, cheaper, more 'colourful' and stop at more stations, every day. Second class fares are cheap: around US$5 for Bulawayo to Harare or Victoria Falls. First class (in compartments) is about double the second class fare. Check at stations for arrival and departure times. Seats can usually be reserved in advance. A railway timetable is available at Harare station or the Tourist Information Office. (Note that Mafeking is spelt Mafikeng on some maps.) This is a great country for railway buffs; many of the trains have steam locos.

Chris and Emma Tatton, two travellers from Britain, wrote to say: *The overnight steam train from Victoria Falls to Bulawayo is a must. We took a first class compartment which was almost luxurious and very reasonably priced. The food in the buffet car was also very good value.*

Boat A car and passenger ferry sails on Lake Kariba, between Kariba town and Mlibizi. Sailings depend on the season, but it's usually once every three days in each direction, and take about 24 hours.

The ferry is used mainly by people with vehicles, as getting to and from Mlibizi is difficult without a car, but it can save you a long trip round if you're travelling direct from Kariba or Mana Pools to Victoria Falls or Hwange. It is easier to go east to west as you may be able to arrange a lift on the ferry to take you away from Mlibizi.

Vehicles need reservations (sometimes months in advance) but foot passengers can just turn up.

Air Air Zimbabwe's internal flights link Harare with other major towns and tourist destinations around the country and can be very useful if your time is short and your budget not too tight. One of the most popular flights for visitors is between Harare and Victoria Falls, which goes via Hwange and Kariba (where you can stop-over for no extra cost). The one-way fare is about US$75 and this flight is worth considering as Hwange is difficult to reach by public transport and the overland route between Vic Falls and Kariba can be very slow without your own vehicle.

Car hire We've heard from some travellers who report that renting a car may be worth considering, even if your budget is tight, as most companies offer weekend discounts which can be quite reasonable if divided between four or five people, or if you've changed money at an unofficial rate. Hertz and Avis have offices in Harare centre and at the airport, and in some other towns. For cheaper rates try Fleet Car Hire at Mike Harris Car Sales, or Truck and Car Hire, both in Harare centre.

Accommodation

All the main towns have large, expensive, good quality hotels, plus a selection of medium and low-range hotels which are more used to catering for travellers on a low budget. (For full details see the individual town descriptions in the next chapter.)

The cheapest hotels in any town are in the townships, or around the bus and train stations. Many of these have noisy bars attached, or may even double as brothels, and are not for the faint-hearted.

All the main towns, national parks and reserves and other tourist centres have campsites usually charging about US$3 per person per night. National park campsites are clean and well-maintained, with clean drinking water, toilets, hot showers, fireplaces and guards. Most city campsites are also good, although some are a bit dilapidated.

Most national parks also have chalets, cottages and lodges for rent, with furniture, beds with sheets and blankets, fridge and cooking facilities (fireplace or stove). Chalets have outside communal cooking and washing facilities. Cottages and lodges have bathroom and kitchen attached. Lodges are also equipped with crockery and cutlery. Prices are very reasonable, normally around US$4 for a double chalet, US$6 for a double cottage and US$8 for a double lodge. (All prices are per person.) Booking for accommodation in national parks is usually required, especially during weekends and school holidays (Christmas and August). But at other times you may be lucky and find accommodation available. Advance bookings for accommodation in any park can be made at the National Parks Central Booking Office, 93b Jason Moyo (Stanley) Ave, Harare, or at the National Parks Booking Agency, 140a Fife St, Bulawayo.

Maps and tourist information

Good quality maps are available from the Public Map Sales Office, Surveyor General, Electra House, Samora Machel Ave, Harare. If you're doing any serious hiking, a map of the area is very useful.

Each major town has an Information Bureau or Tourist Office, administered by the local Publicity Association. Although they do not usually cater for budget travellers, the staff are normally friendly and helpful, and can provide informative maps and leaflets about all the national parks, reserves and tourist sites in the surrounding area.

In Harare and (to a lesser extent) Bulawayo are several travel and tour agents who can arrange international or domestic flights, bus and train bookings, hotel accommodation, safaris, rafting and so on. There are also several tour agents at Victoria Falls.

Chapter Two

Cities and Towns

Since independence a number of towns in Zimbabwe have changed their name, either abandoning a European name and introducing an African one, or Africanising the spelling. Street names, in all towns, are frequently revised. In this book former names are shown in brackets. Ask at an Information Bureau for a map and list of recent changes. Towns that have changed are:

Old Name	New Name	Old Name	New Name
Belingwe	Mberengwa	Melsetter	Chimanimani
Chipinga	Chipinge	Mrewa	Murewa
Dett	Dete	Mtoko	Mutoko
Essexvale	Esigodini	Nuanetsi	Mwenezi
Enkeldoorn	Chivhu	Que Que	Kwe Kwe
Fort Victoria/ Nyanda	Masvingo	Salisbury	Harare
		Selukwe	Shurugwe
Gatooma	Kadoma	Shabani	Zvishavane
Gwelo	Gweru	Sinoia	Chinhoyi
Hartley	Chegutu	Sipolilo	Guruwe
Inyanga	Nyanga	Tjolotjo	Tsholotsho
Inyazura	Nyazura	Umtali	Mutare
Mangula	Mhangura	Vila Salazar	Sango
Marandellas	Marondera	Vumba	Bvumba
Mashaba	Mashava	Wankie	Hwange

The names of several national parks have also been revised. In this book these are:

Inyanga	Nyanga	Matopos	Matobo
Wankie	Hwange		

Cities and Towns

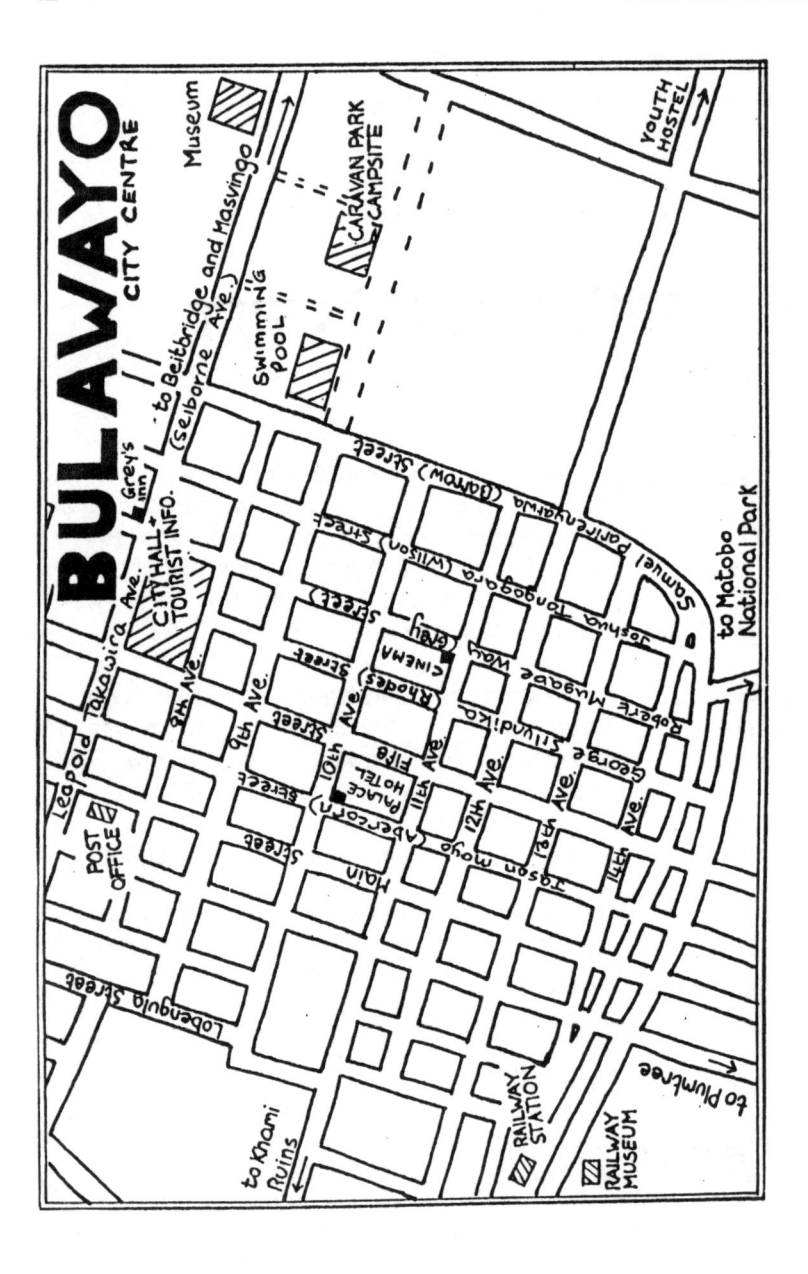

Bulawayo

Bulawayo is one of Zimbabwe's oldest European settlements, built on the site of the 'kraal' (compound) of Lobengula, the last king of the Matabele. It is now the second largest town in Zimbabwe. The town has many links with Cecil Rhodes, the original founder of Rhodesia. The main streets in the town centre are remarkably wide. This was so that in colonial days there was room for wagons with a team of oxen to turn completely around.

The Publicity Bureau, in the City Hall, is very helpful and can provide maps and information on Bulawayo and the surrounding area.

Coming and going

Bulawayo is linked to Harare and Victoria Falls by train and bus, with daily services at least once in each direction. Buses also run to and from Masvingo. There are international train services to and from Francistown (Botswana) and Johannesburg (South Africa).

Places to stay

The excellent **campsite** at The Caravan Park, on the east side of town, 15 minutes walk from the centre, has hot showers, firewood and guards for Z$10 per site.

The **Youth Hostel**, near the junction of 12th Ave and 3rd St, outside the city centre, is pleasant and the cheapest place to stay at Z$20 per person. Reasonably priced hotels include the **Palace Hotel** and **Grand Hotel** (about Z$80 per double), both on Jason Moyo (Abercorn) St, between 10th and 11th. More expensive, but popular with travellers and good value, is **Grey's Inn** (Z$120 perdouble) on Robert Mugabe Way (Grey St), near the junction of Leopold Takawira (Selborne) Ave.

Places to visit

Museums The **National Natural History Museum** is modern, well organised and very interesting. The museum contains more than just natural history though: there's plenty of other exhibits contrasting African and colonial European cultures. The **Railway Museum** near the station is interesting for train buffs.

Khami Ruins Twenty kilometres west of Bulawayo, off a small road which goes to the village of Soluksi, are the ruins of Khami, second in archaeological importance only to the ruins of Great Zimbabwe. The impressive terraces, passages and walls were constructed in the 17th century by the pre-colonial inhabitants of this area.

Tshabalala Sanctuary Just outside Bulawayo on the road to the Matobo National Park, this is an ideal game park for travellers without a vehicle as you are permitted to walk here. However, you need to be very quiet and patient if you want to see any wild life, although the park does contain giraffe, kudu, zebra, wildebeest and many species of water bird.

Chipangali Wildlife Orphanage About 20km from Bulawayo on the Johannesburg road. Various injured or abandoned animals. (Closed Mondays.)

Matobo National Park About 50km to the south of Bulawayo, this is a great area for hiking or simply strolling around for a few days. For more details see Chapter Three.

Harare

Harare is a modern capital with a clean and spacious city centre, complete with office blocks, paved shopping streets, restaurants and department stores.

For information about Harare and the surrounding area visit the Publicity Association Information Bureau on Second Street in African Unity Square (Cecil Square), a small park in the city centre. Nearby is the Zimbabwe Tourist Board office (for general tourist information), on the corner of Jason Moyo (Stanley) Ave and 4th Street; and the National Parks HQ (for information and accommodation bookings in the parks), at 93b Jason Moyo (Stanley) Ave.

The map of Harare (opposite) shows only the essentials in the city centre. Detailed maps of the whole city are available from the Publicity Association Information Bureau.

Coming and going

Harare is linked to Bulawayo and Mutare by bus and train, with daily services at least once in each direction. Express buses leave from Rezende Street, between Leopold Takawira Street and Julius

Harare 15

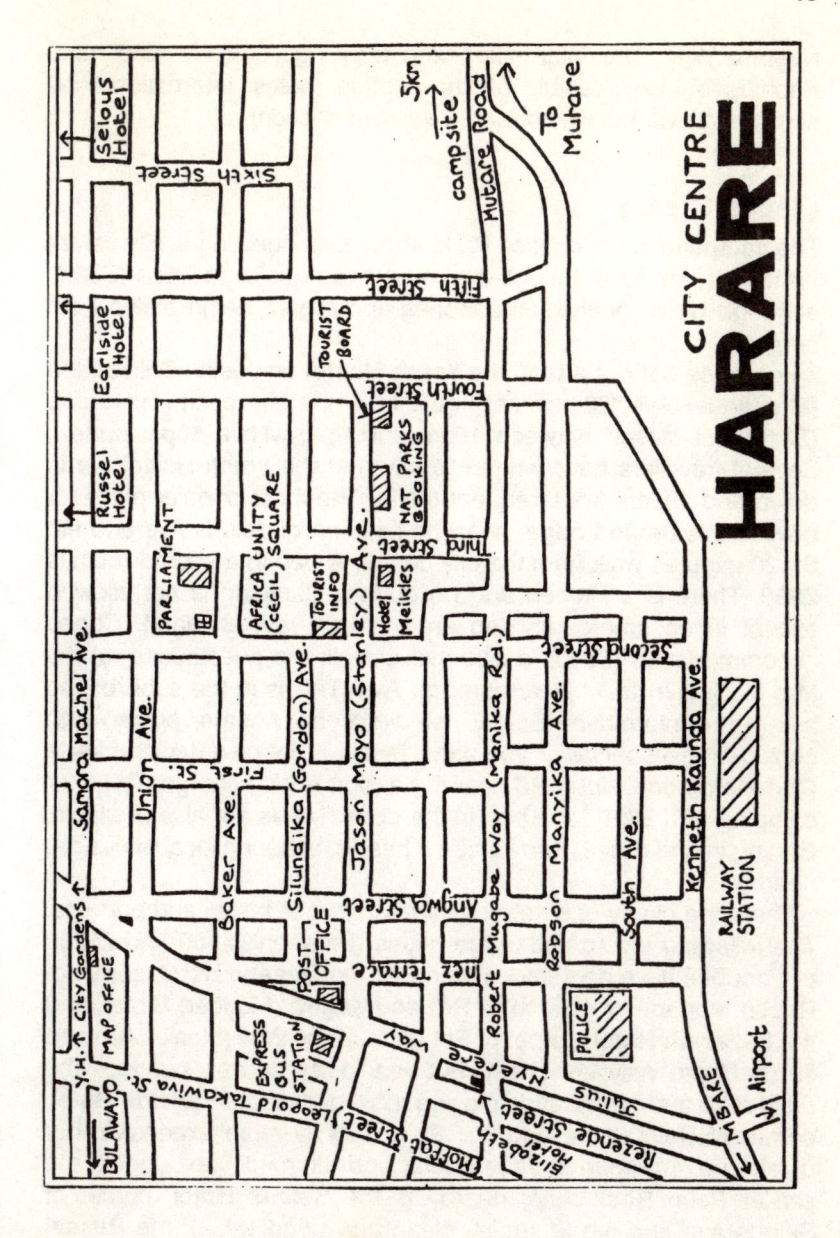

Nyerere Way. The information and bookings office is also here. Hitching is also possible on these main routes. International rail services go via Bulawayo (see Bulawayo section).

Places to stay

The **campsite** at Coronation Park, about 5km outside the city centre on the Mutare road, has all the usual good-quality facilities (Z$20), although we've heard some stories about gear being stolen from here.

For those without a tent, the **Youth Hostel** on Josiah Chinamano (Montague) Ave, 20 minutes' walk from the city centre, is cheap (Z$10) but closed between 10am and 5pm with a 10pm curfew. Several travellers have written to say that the Youth Hostel is run down and suffers from frequent thefts. The most popular place for travellers is **Sable Lodge**, near the junction of Selous Ave and 9th St, 20 minutes walk from the city centre. A bed in a shared room is Z$50. There is a kitchen and no curfew. Camping is not allowed except in an emergency (eg arriving very late at night). Cheap accommodation (Z$40) is also available at the guesthouse run by Mrs McCraken at 11 Peterborough Ave. This is in the suburbs, so ask at the Information Bureau for directions. Another place worth considering, especially if you arrive by air, is the new **Backpacker's Con-x-sion** on Delport Rd near the airport, which charges Z$20 for camping and Z$50 for a bed in the dorm. Meals are also available. Getting in and out of town can be a hassle, although local buses run nearby.

There are plenty of hotels in Harare to suit all tastes and budgets. The following low to mid-range hotels (between Z$100 and Z$200 per double) have been recommended: the **Queens Hotel**, corner of Robert Mugabe Way (Manica Rd) and Kaguvi (Pioneer) Street, and the **Elizabeth Hotel**, corner of Robert Mugabe Way (Manica Rd) and Julius Nyere Way are cheap but very noisy as they overlook the main road and have bands playing most nights; the **Earlside Hotel**, corner of Selous Ave and 5th St, is slightly more expensive, but quiet, in a suburban street, popular and often full; next door is the similar **Palm Rock Villa**; nearby is the **Selous Hotel**, corner of Selous Ave and 6th St (quiet, clean and good value); the **Russel Hotel**, corner of Bains Ave and Third St, is more expensive again but generally has room. If the cheaper hotels are full, you may have to reserve a room for the following night and spend one night in a slightly more expensive place.

Places to visit

The **National Museum** on the edge of the city centre, towards the Sheraton Hotel, has some informative wildlife displays, showing you what you should be seeing in the game reserves and national parks, and the **National Gallery**, near the big Monamatapa Hotel, has some fascinating displays of traditional and very modern Zimbabwean art.

The **Muzika market** in Mbare Township next to the long distance bus terminal is a colourful African market.

Lake McIlwaine Recreational Park, about 30km south-west of Harare is a fenced park with plenty of game (including rhino). Diana Clement (Britain) wrote to us saying: *We had good game-viewing here: eland, topi, kudu, zebra, wildebeest and even rhino, all in a short time. We went riding on some very energetic horses. Hitching to the park was easy and we stayed in cheap chalets.* Neil Irving (Britain) writes: *Avoid the zoo and lion park on the way; they're the worst I've ever seen for animals caged in small pens.*

For **nightclubs** and places with music, get a copy of *What's on in Harare* available from the Tourist Office.

Warning

The **president's house** is on Chancellor Avenue, on the northern outskirts of the city. All roads around the house are closed between 6pm and 6am every night for security reasons. Guards will shoot anybody who disregards this regulation.

Useful addresses

British High Commission,
Stanley House, Jason Moyo Avenue
PO Box 4490. Tel: 793781.

United States of America Embassy
172 Herbert Chitepo Ave
PO Box 3340. Tel: 794521.

Australia High Commission
Karigamombe Centre, Samora Machel Avenue
Tel: 794591.

South Africa Embassy
Temple Bar House, Beker Ave
Tel: 707901.

Botswana High Commission,
Southern Life Building, Jason Moyo Ave
Tel: 729551.

There are also embassies of the following African countries in Harare which issue visas: Kenya, Mozambique, Nigeria, South Africa, Tanzania, Zaire, Zambia.

Kariba

Kariba is most famous for its dam, built across the Zambezi River to create Lake Kariba, one of the largest artificial lakes in Africa. The nearby town of Kariba was originally built to house the dam construction workers. Today the town and this part of the lake shore is a holiday resort - the nearest thing that Zimbabwe has to the seaside! Several canoe and rafting safari outfits are also based here.

If you're travelling to or from Zambia on the Lusaka-Harare road (ie missing Victoria Falls), it's worth turning off the main road (at Makuti in Zimbabwe or the Siavonga turn-off in Zambia) and crossing the border at Kariba.

Places to stay

The town of Kariba is on top of the hill overlooking the lake. Several expensive hotels line the lake shore below. There are two campsites, both with chalets: **Mopani Bay Caravan Park** is about 6km from the dam about 1km off the road to/from Makuti; the **Moth Campsite** is more central, nearer the dam and ferry dock, and with shops and a small market at the nearby township.

For a cool beer or a 'splash out' meal in luxurious surroundings overlooking the lake, campers at Mopani Bay can stroll along to the nearby Cutty Sark Hotel, while those at the Moth Campsite can walk up the steep path to the Lake View Hotel.

Places to visit

The **Kariba Dam** is open to visitors, a few kilometres walk or hitch from the town and lake shore. The Zambezi River divides Zimbabwe

Kariba

and Zambia, so unless you're actually crossing here, you can only go half way along the top of the dam. There's a notice board with some information, and the views down the gorge below the dam are superb. Look out for crocodiles swimming around in the water below the outlet pipes.

Kariba is also the centre for visiting **Matusadona National Park**, on the lake shore to the south of Kariba town, and **Mana Pools National Park**, about 80km to the north-east, bordering the southern side of the Zambezi River. Matusadona and Mana Pools are 'wild' parks, both reknowned for their dramatic scenery and spectacular wildlife, including lion, leopard, elephant, buffalo, hippo and crocodile. For more details on these parks, see Chapter Four, *Places of Interest*.

Masvingo

Formerly Fort Victoria, this town is nothing special in itself. There are a couple of expensive hotels and a good **Caravan Park**/campsite, with all facilities, for Z$10 per person per night, about 1km from the centre of town, on the road to Mutare.

Places to visit

The main reason to come to Masvingo is to travel on to the nearby Lake Kyle Recreation Park or Great Zimbabwe ruins.

Lake Kyle Recreation Park This is a small park overlooking the lake. The entrance is about 20km south-east of Masvingo off the Masvingo-Mutare road. There's a quiet, peaceful campsite with all the usual facilities, and lodges too. You can easily hitch to the campsite, but you need your own vehicle to go around the game reserve. You might be able to hitch a ride with other tourists or with the game wardens. You can hire horses here or boats to go out onto the lake. It's also possible to hire a boat to take you across to the Great Zimbabwe Ruins which are on the other side of the lake.

The Great Zimbabwe Ruins The largest pre-colonial stone structure south of the Sahara, this mysterious ancient citadel is a high point of any visit to Zimbabwe. See Chapter Four, *Places of Interest*.

Mutare

Mutare is regarded as Zimbabwe's third city (after Harare and Bulawayo) even though the town of Gweru — in the Midlands — is also larger. Mutare is the 'capital' of the eastern region of Manicaland, and most travellers pass through here on their way to the Eastern Highlands. Mutare has a market, shops and supermarkets and a very good Information Bureau in the city centre.

Coming and going

Mutare is linked to Harare by train and bus with daily (or overnight) services. (It is also possible to hitch from Harare, especially at weekends.) Mutare bus station is in Sakubva township, a few km beyond the city centre, but coming in from Harare all buses stop in the centre first. From Sakubva buses go to Nyanga and Chimanimani in the Eastern Highlands.

Places to stay

The cheapest hotel in Mutare is the **Balmoral Hotel** (Z$60, double). Some travellers have also written to us about Ann Bruce's small guesthouse, in the residential area just outside the city centre, with rooms for Z$40. Another place that has been recommended is at 5 Livingstone Rd, with beds for Z$30 and floor space for Z$20. The Information Bureau may be able to give more details. There's also a **campsite** with all the usual facilities for the usual price on Christmas Pass. If you're coming from the direction of Harare it's on the left as you go down the steep hill towards Mutare about 6km before you get into the town proper.

Places to visit

Musems The **Mutare Museum** is well-organised and informative with exhibits on archeology, pre-colonial and post-colonial history, farming and mining, plus an aviary and snake pit. The **Utopia House Museum**, on the edge of the city centre, was originally built by an early colonialist and has now been restored and furnished in the style of the period.

Aloe Garden In the Main Park, at the southern end of the city centre, near the railway station, 243 species of aloe from all over Africa are displayed. They bloom in July, but the garden and park are pleasant places to visit at any time of year.

Mutare

Cecil Kop Nature Reserve On the outskirts of Mutare this small reserve is divided into two parts: Tiger's Kloof Dam and Thompson's Vlei.

The Tiger's Kloof Dam area is almost a zoo but is worth a visit to see the zebras, baboons and rhino at such close quarters. The animals are fed every day at 4 pm and can be viewed from an observation point overlooking the dam. This is a good way of seeing the animals if you don't have a car.

The Thompson's Vlei section of the reserve is a little further outside town and you need a car to go around inside. Part of the reserve runs along the Mozambique border, a huge barbed wire fence punctuated by red skull-and-crossbone signs warning potential trespassers of the danger of minefields. There's very little game but you do get a very good view from the top of Tigers Kloof mountain of the town of Mutare, and over to the mountains of Vumba and Chimanimani.

Bvumba (Vumba) Botanical Gardens and Reserve This is a small reserve with a campsite and short nature trails, about 30km from Mutare. See Chapter Four, *Places of Interest*.

Nyanga National Park This is a large area of mountain 'wilderness' about 150km north of Mutare offering excellent hiking possibilities. See Chapter Three, *Hiking*.

AFRICA TRAVEL SHOP

All the information you will ever need on travel to

- ☺ **Safaris throughout Africa** - Kenya, Tanzania, Zimbabwe, Botswana, Namibia, S. Africa, Zambia, Uganda, Zaire, Rwanda, Ghana, Ethiopia and more.
- ☺ **Overland Expeditions** - All the operators under one roof. Send for our unique *'Guide to Overland Africa'*.
- ☺ **Low Cost Camping Safaris** - The widest range of arrangements available. We have brochures that no other UK travel agent has!
- ☺ **Adventure and Activity Safaris** - Gorilla Treks, White Water Rafting, Kilimanjaro Climbs, Camel Safaris etc.
- ☺ **Tailor-Made Arrangements** - Our expert consultants will enjoy helping you plan a perfect itinerary.

FREE

Don't even think about Africa without your copy of Africa Travel Now. This newspaper is free only from us - packed with information on health, visas, weather, gameparks, public holidays and much more...

AFRICA TRAVEL SHOP
4 Medway Ct,
Leigh St,
London, WC1H
9QX.

Fax: 071 383 7512

Tel:
071 387 1211

Sketched at Cecil Kop, Mutare

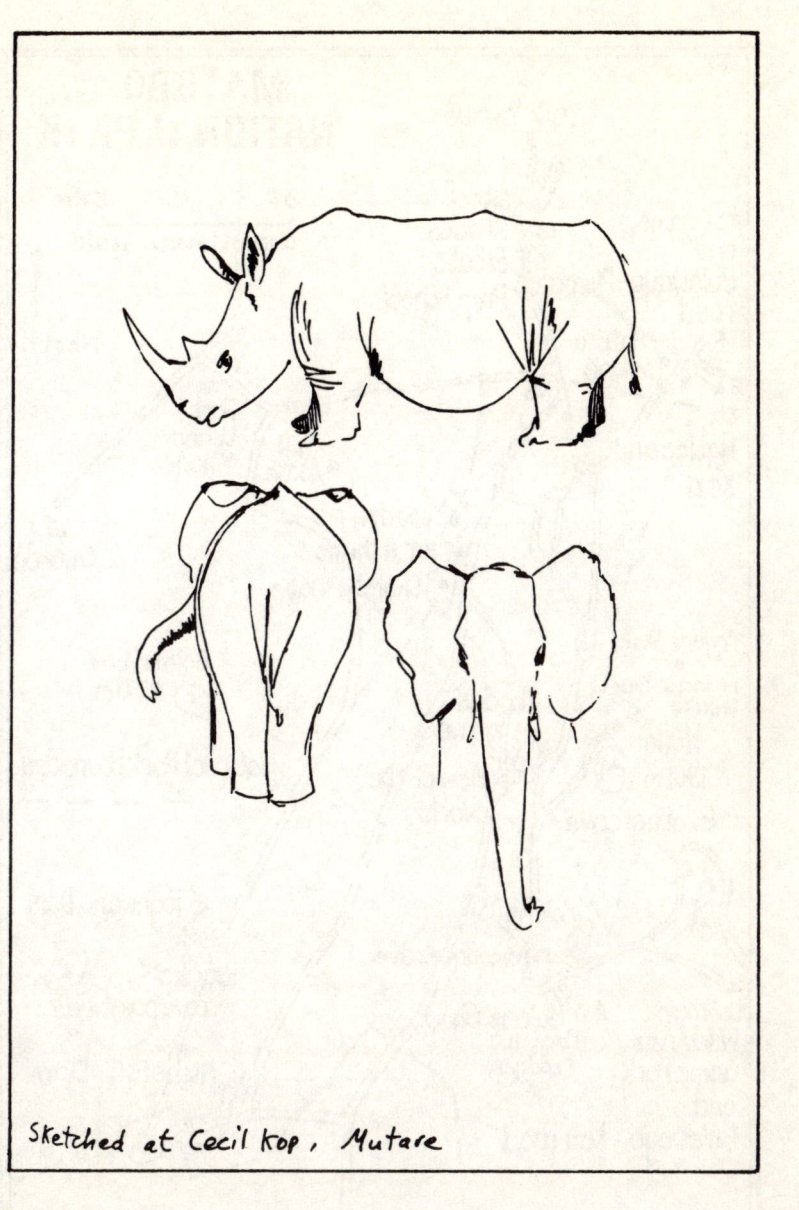

24

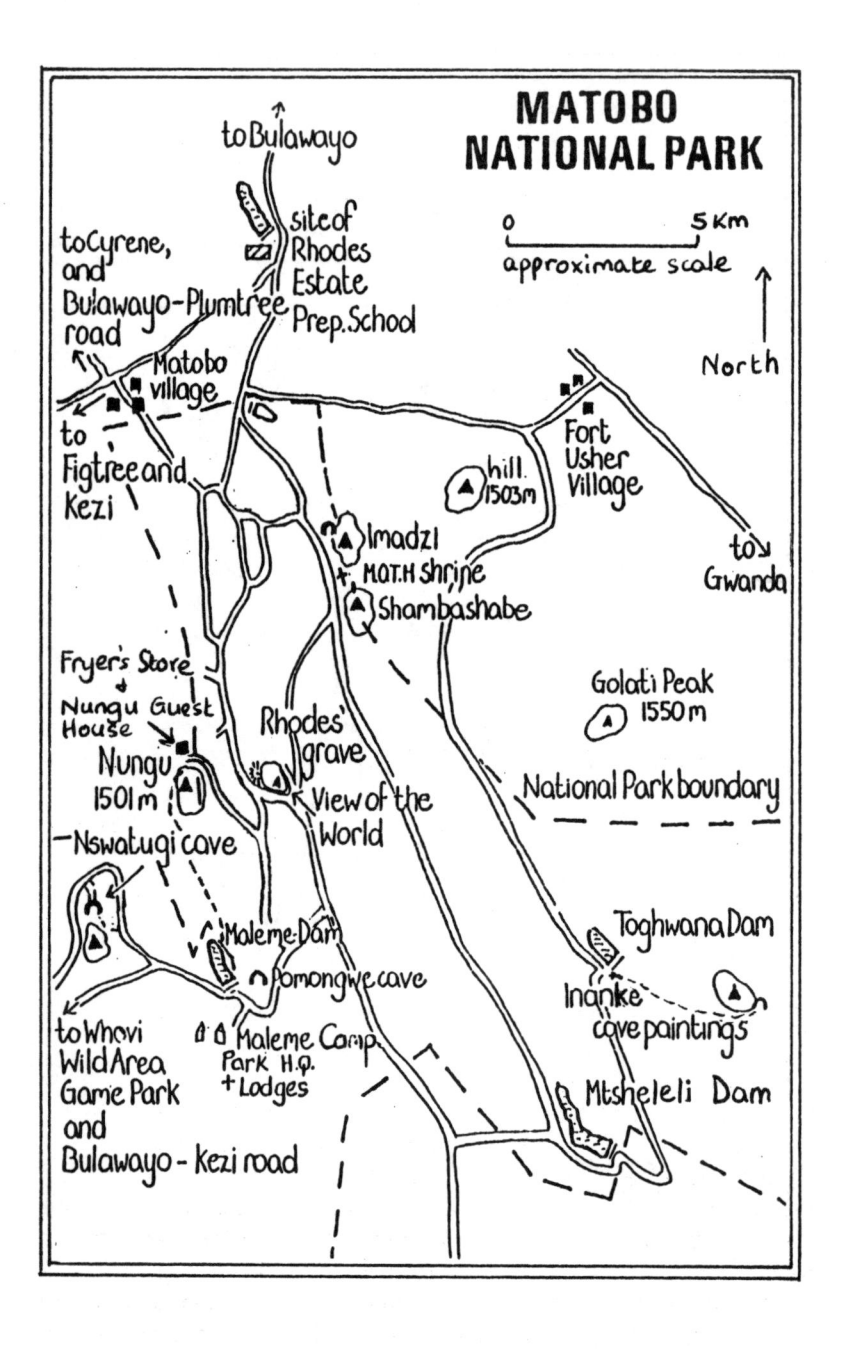

Chapter Three

Hiking

Matobo National Park

The Matobo is a range of low rounded hills covering an area of some 3000 square kilometres in the southeast of Zimbabwe. The summits of most of the hills are bare granite rock, eroded along faultlines over millions of years to form either smooth domed 'whalebacks' or tall 'kopjies' of towers and pillars, often capped by standing boulders.

The area has been inhabited for many thousands of years: several caves contain good examples of ancient 'bushman' painting. The Matobos were sacred to the Shona people, and to the Matabele people who came after them; the maze of hills and valleys made an ideal refuge in times of war. Several Matabele chiefs were buried in the Matobo Hills and Cecil John Rhodes, the founder of Rhodesia (later to become Zimbabwe) chose one of the highest hills to be the site of his own grave.

The Matabele gave the area its current name: *matobo* means 'bald-head', referring to the dome-shaped hills. This was corrupted by early European settlers, and the hills were known as The Matopos. The original African spelling has now been reintroduced.

To protect this area of cultural importance, and the wildlife it contains, a section has been gazetted as a national park, covering some 450 square kilometres, divided into four separate areas. The Whovi Wild Area, in the west of the park, contains several species, including rhino, giraffe, eland, zebra, kudu and waterbuck. This area can only be entered in a vehicle, but the rest of the park can be reached without a car and is an excellent area for hiking.

You can base yourself at one of the pleasant campsites, and hike in the park, following tracks and footpaths through grassy valleys or across the bald summits of some of the larger hills, to visit ancient cave paintings or more recent burial sites. Treading quietly, you will probably see some of the Matobo's wildlife (often missed by car drivers), such as sable antelope, waterbuck or klipspringer. And you can be as noisy as you like, and still see the baboons in their colonies at the top of some of the rock towers. Birds are also abundant: the Matobo Hills contain over half of all the species found in Zimbabwe.

Getting there

Matobo National Park is near Bulawayo, Zimbabwe's second city (see Chapter Two for more details).

Matobo is easy for drivers to reach. From Bulawayo a signposted road leads straight to the Matobo National Park, tarred as far as Maleme Camp, the park HQ and main accommodation centre (54km).

Most of the hiking routes described in this section start from Maleme. There is no public transport to Maleme itself but the bus to Kezi passes the junction about 30km from Bulawayo where the tarred road leads to Maleme. Hitching is possible from here, especially at weekends, or from the outskirts of Bulawayo.

Alternatively, you can take the Kezi bus as far as Whitewaters Dam, on the western side of the park, near the entrance to Whovi Wild Area, and from there walk the 9km to Maleme Camp. (There's a small campsite at Whitewaters Dam.)

Places to stay

Travellers without a car should aim for Maleme Camp, as this is the easiest place to reach. Maleme Camp, which is also the park HQ, has lodges (Z$60 per person per night) and chalets (Z$40 per person per night), plus a campsite at Maleme Dam (10 minutes walk from Maleme Camp). There are also campsites at Mtsheleli Dam and Toghwana Dam: all have water supply (treated at Maleme), toilets and hot showers. All campsites cost Z$20. Camping is only allowed at designated sites. Reservations for lodges and chalets, often necessary at weekends, can be made in advance at the National Park Central Booking Office in Harare, or at the National Parks Booking Office in Bulawayo.

Another option is Inungu Guest House, a fully contained and serviced cottage attached to Fryer's Store, just outside the park boundary (details below). Rates start at about Z$200 per night, for

Matobo National Park

up to four people. Reservations can be made through Sunshine Tours, Old Mutual Building, Bulawayo, Tel: 67791.

Getting organised

There is no shop at Maleme Camp, or anywhere in the park. The nearest place for supplies is Fryer Store, just outside the park, about 12km by track from Maleme, or about two hours' walk along footpaths, but supplies here are sometimes limited to Cokes, biscuits and a few items of tinned food. It's best to bring most of what you need from Bulawayo.

The park is covered by the official Map of Matobo National Park (at a scale of 1:50,000). This is available in Bulawayo or from the map office in Harare. The Information Bureau in Bulawayo sometimes has tourist maps, which are less detailed but still adequate.

Visitors to the national park must pay entrance fees on top of camping fees. These are Z$20 for one day, Z$40 for up to seven days.

HIKING ROUTES

The park does not contain many paths specifically for hiking, but most of the park's tracks are rarely used by vehicles, especially on weekdays, and are fine for walking.

Of the hiking paths that do exist, most are clearly marked by white arrows painted on the rock. This detracts from the feel of wilderness, but is often necessary as some paths are indistinct.

Maleme Dam to Nswatugi Cave

This 10km route is a good 'starter'. It is straightforward and a notice board near the cave provides useful background information on the geological formation and history of the Matobo Hills, the original 'Bushman' inhabitants, the cave paintings and the wildlife found in the park.

N.B. In Southern Africa a 'dam' is what other English-speaking people would call a 'reservoir'. What the Brits call a 'dam' is called a 'dam wall'. The difference can cause confusion: for a Zimbabwean 'To walk across a dam' implies supernatural powers!

From Maleme Campsite, follow the track over the dam wall and along the southern side of the dam to fork right at a junction. Continue on the track through an area of kopjies and rock towers to reach a crossroads, with Madingizulu Dam visible 100m to the right. Turn left and follow the track as it winds up between domes and cliffs to reach the cave site. A ranger is based here and will lead you up the last section of steep footpath to the cave itself.

You can return by the same route, or continue on tracks, past Mesilume Dam and the entrance to Whovi Wild Area, to turn left and follow the (signposted) track back to Maleme. Alternatively, the ranger will show you the start of the short cut path back to the track from Maleme, and the route can be retraced from there.

Maleme Dam to Pomongwe Hill and Cave

Pomongwe Hill is a classic domed 'whaleback' and one of the largest hills in the area. Views from the top are particularly good at sunset so this short route (taking between one and two hours) is best done in the evening.

From opposite the Maleme Camp and park HQ entrance, a path (clearly marked by white arrows) leads straight up to the top. About halfway up, the path divides: the left path leads to the summit; the right path leads over smooth rock and beside the edge a rounded cliff down to Pomongwe Cave, larger than Nswatugi, but with less distinctive paintings.

Maleme Dam to The View of the World

This all-day walk (taking about 6 to 8 hours), follows paths and tracks, and includes several of the park's main points of interest, including the giant Nungu cross, Rhodes' Grave at the View of the World, Laing's Graveyard and Pomongwe Cave.

From Maleme Dam take the track through the campsite, keeping the dam to your left. The large dome of Nungu Hill, with the cross on the summit, is visible directly ahead. After 45 minutes you reach a fork; turn right to reach a grassy clearing at the foot of Nungu's southern slopes. From here a path leads up the hill, following white arrows and occasional cairns, across bare rock and through patches of bush. Near the summit, at a point below a small cliff, another path joins from the left. Keep straight on, to scramble up a large crack, with the help of some metal pegs, to reach easier ground and the giant cross on the summit. The views from this point are spectacular.

Matobo National Park

From the cross retrace to the foot of the small cliff then fork right and follow the other path which leads down and right, towards the northern side of Nungu Hill. Follow the white arrows (pointing up the hill), down through woodland until the path becomes a driveable track. Continue on the track to a junction marked by an oil-drum. Turn right and follow this track to a fork. Keep right to meet another track near a fence and gate marking the boundary of the park.

Turn right onto this track (left goes to Fryer's Store), through the gate, to re-enter the park and meet another track, the 'Scenic Route' between the Circular Drive and Maleme. Turn left and follow this track through woodland to meet the tarred Circular Drive. Turn right on to the tarred road which crosses a small drainage tunnel marked by four small white concrete posts (two on either side of the road). Continue for about 75m to find a faint footpath on the left, about 10m before another set of white posts. Follow this path through a strip of woodland and then steeply up over bare rock, bearing right nearer the top, through light bush, to reach a carpark and picnic site. A clear path leads from the carpark up to Rhodes' Grave on the highest point of the hill.

The hill is called Malindidzimu, 'the place of the spirits' (a sacred site for the Matabele where several chiefs are also buried), but is more commonly known as the View of the World (Rhodes' own name for the hill). In the carpark is an information board with a history of Rhodes' life and photographs of his burial ceremony. The grave itself is marked by a simple stone slab, in accordance with his wishes. Nearby is the grave of Leander Starr Jameson (Rhodes' second-in-command) and the large square monument to Alan Wilson, and the 'Brave Men' of the Shangani Patrol, who died in a battle with Matabele warriors in 1893.

From Rhodes' Grave, retrace the footpath to the Circular Drive on the west side of Malindidzimu, and follow the Scenic Route back to the junction where the track turns off right to Fryer's Store. Keep straight on here, passing through open grassland, to reach Laing's Graveyard on the right of the track, the site of another battle between British soldiers and Matabele warriors. A plaque on the rock tells the story.

Continue on the track to reach a junction and turn right onto the main park road. Turn right onto a dirt road to reach Pomongwe Cave. On the right side of the track, 100m before the cave, a very steep path goes up the cliff, marked by white arrows, over the side of Pomongwe Hill to reach Maleme.

Toghwana Dam to Inange Cave

Inange Cave (also spelt Inanke) contains some of the best preserved cave paintings in Zimbabwe. The path to the cave starts at Toghwana Dam, in the southeastern part of the park.

If you don't have a car, from Maleme to Toghwana is a 22km walk along tracks, but this is not strenuous and passes though some small settlements (outside the park boundary) on the way. You might be able to hitch a ride from Maleme, or you could backpack there and spend a night camping at Toghwana before visiting the caves the following day.

The path to the cave passes through spectacular countryside, over broad open ridges overlooking swampy basins and along vegetated valleys below steep cliffs where eagles' nests (and sometimes the birds themselves) can be seen. The path is clearly marked by white arrows and is easy to follow until the last section where it circles back on itself to avoid scrambling up almost sheer cliffs below the site of the cave. Allow about two hours, each way, to do the walk, plus time to see the cave and take in the spectacular scenery.

Gail Davey (Britain) did this route and wrote: *The cave at Inange is by far the most inspiring in Matobo. There are hundreds of figures and symbols at various levels on the back wall of the cave. (The paintings are far better than those at Pomongwe Cave, which were 'preserved' with glycerine earlier this century, and almost entirely erased.)*

If you want to take a break from walking, horses can be hired from Maleme Camp park office. An early morning ride is very enjoyable and you may see a lot of game. A guide comes with you.

Margaret Cullum from Britain writes: *In my opinion, one of the highlights of Zimbabwe is Matobo. We cheated getting there, by taking a one day safari with a great chap called Russel Pumfrey (bookable through the Tourist Office in Bulawayo), then stayed on a few days, hitching out. We waited half a day to get a lift out, and were told later you need to be on the road by 9 a.m. to have a good chance of getting a lift.*

The Nyanga Mountains

The Nyanga Mountains form the northern part of the Eastern Highlands, the long range that marks Zimbabwe's border with Mozambique. They include Mount Nyangani, Zimbabwe's highest

The Nyanga Mountains

Taking a break from walking...!
Here we go again....!

mountain at 2592m (8504ft), plus several other peaks, divided by deep valleys and the dramatic Pungwe Gorge.

The mountains have been inhabited since earliest times by various peoples. Remains of the stone fortifications and terracing can still be seen on hilltops and valley sides. In the early part of the 20th Century the Eastern Highlands, with a landscape and climate like many parts of northern Europe, was a popular place for settlers from Britain and South Africa.

Cecil John Rhodes, the founder of Rhodesia, owned land in this area which was given to the country on his death and gazetted as the Rhodes Inyanga National Park. The name was changed after Zimbabwe became independent in 1980. Today the area is a popular holiday destination for residents and visitors, who come for the fine scenery, cool air, fishing and golf, as well as for the pleasant and varied hiking.

Getting there

Nyanga town is the nearest settlement to the national park, reached from Harare (300km), via Rusape, or from Mutare (110km). Express buses link Harare, Rusape and Mutare, and local buses run between Mutare, Rusape and Nyanga town. It is also possible to hitch on these roads.

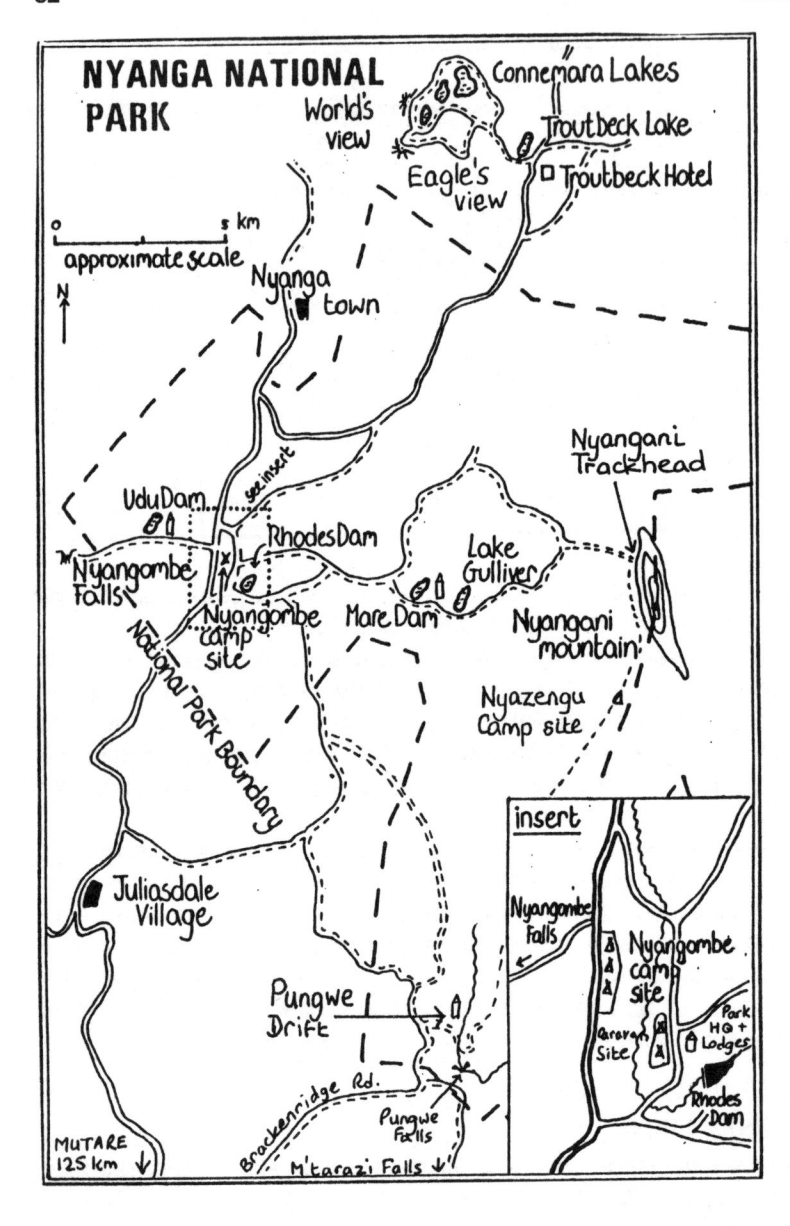

Hiking

The Nyanga Mountains

Places to stay

Most travellers stay at Nyangombe Campsite (formerly Inyangombe), on the right side of the main road from Mutare, about 10km south of Nyanga town. This is near the park HQ, and is a pleasant site amongst pine trees with a guard, toilets, hot showers and laundry facilities, all for Z$20 per night.

Camping is also possible at Nyazengu Campsite, on a small area of private land surrounded by the park, on the southwestern slopes of Mount Nyangani. The campsite has limited facilities (toilet and tap) and can only be reached by foot or 4WD, but it commands an excellent view of the surrounding country, and is a useful stopover if you're doing the Nyangani to Pungwe Drift Route described in this section. A marked circular day-walk (5-7 hours) starting from the campsite and going up to the ridge south of Nyangani is also available. More information is available from the Park HQ. Camping is not allowed anywhere else in the park.

If you're looking for solid accommodation, the national park also has lodges at Rhodes Dam, Mare Dam and Udu Dam (Z$100 per lodge for 2/3 people, Z$150 for 4/5, Z$200 for 8). Reservations (often necessary at weekends and holidays) can be made at the National Parks Central Booking Office in Harare. At other times the lodges are unlikely to be full; check for space at the park HQ, near Rhodes Dam, when you arrive.

In the surrounding area are several hotels, catering mainly for the more wealthy Zimbabweans and tourists, and rarely used by budget travellers. A possibility, if you fancy a splurge, is the Rhodes Nyanga Hotel, formerly Rhodes' own house, a small hotel in the best position for hikers. A small museum is attached. Double rooms start at about Z$250 half-board and gents must wear ties in the evening. Prices are about the same, but attire is less formal, at the Nyanga Holiday Hotel in Nyanga town.

Getting organised

For supplies, there are small shops at Juliasdale, Troutbeck and Nyanga town (which also has a market). The shops in Mutare have a wider selection.

The Tourist Map of Nyanga National Park marks all roads, tracks, dams and places of interest in the park. If this is not available, other survey maps of the area are available from the map office in Harare. More basic, but adequate, maps of the area may be available from the Tourist Office in Mutare.

Even if you stay outside the park, you are supposed to pay national park entrance fees when you walk here. These are: Z$20 for visits of less than one day; Z$40 for up to seven days.

If you don't have camping equipment or the inclination to walk alone in the Eastern Highlands, a small outfit called Howard Barnes Trails organises hikes and treks in the area. Rates start at Z$200 per day, including transport, food, park fees, and guide. For more information contact Howard Barnes, 154 Upper East Rd, PO Box A146, Avondale, Harare, Tel Harare 304339, or Mutare 217129.

HIKING ROUTES

The hiking here is potentially more serious than in the Matobo. Local legend tells that this mountain 'eats' people and some hikers have been seriously lost in the past when mists obscured the route. The path to the summit should not be attempted if visibility is bad. You don't need any special equipment to walk here: training shoes are adaquate but you should carry warm clothing and waterproofs, especially in the wet season.

Nyangombe Campsite to Mount Nyangani

On the eastern boundary of Nyanga National Park, Mount Nyangani (formerly Inyangani) is the highest peak in the Nyanga range, and in Zimbabwe. Viewed from the park side (the west) the mountain does not look particularly high or impressive but it is much steeper on its eastern side, dropping sharply towards the plains of Mozambique. Views from the summit are dramatic in both directions, weather permiting. The walk takes about eight hours, there and back, although you may be lucky and hitch a ride some of the way along the park track.

From Nyangombe Campsite follow the park track, signposted, past the turn-off on the right to the ruins of Nyangwe Fort, to reach Mare Dam (pronounced Ma-re). Continue past the dam and lodges to reach a junction after 7km. Turn right, then almost immediately fork right to reach another fork: right is signposted 'Private Road'; keep left to reach the 'trackhead' (end of the track), 14km or about three hours walk from Nyangombe

From the trackhead, follow the clear path steeply up, marked by cairns and white arrows, to reach the crest of the ridge. Follow the yellow-topped cairns, past the 'keep going' sign, to reach the white beacon that marks the summit (2594m) after another one to two

The Nyanga Mountains

hours (depending on your rate of ascent).

From the summit the ridge extends southwards towards two lower peaks with Tucker's Gap (obscured) between them. To the northeast, the dark sides of Little Nyangani can be seen across the Gairezi Valley. To the north, the World's View escarpment beyond Troutbeck is visible, topped by the Connemara Lakes and a radio mast, while directly below, the track leading towards Pungwe Drift can be clearly seen following the broad ridge towards the southwest.

Allow about 45 minutes for the descent to the trackhead by the same route. From here you can retrace the route back to Nyangombe. Alternatively, you can continue along the track to Pungwe Drift, camping one or two nights on the way, following the route described below.

Nyangani Trackhead to Pungwe Drift

This 22km route passes through some of the most spectacular scenery in this part of the Eastern Highlands but, unless you arrange 'solid' accommodation at Pungwe Drift (details below), you need to be self-contained for at least one night's camping on the way. Camping is not allowed on national park land, but it is permitted at Nyazengu Campsite, described in the *Places to stay* section above.

Warning At Pungwe Drift this route fords a large river, usually less than knee-deep, but which may be impassable after heavy rain. You should not attempt to cross this river if it is in flood. Either retrace the entire route, or follow the river upstream (possibly for several hours) until a suitable crossing point can be reached.

To reach the Nyangani Trackhead, follow the directions above. (It is possible to walk from Nyangombe, up to Nyangani summit and then to Nyazengu Campsite in one day.)

From the trackhead, retrace 300m to the 'Private Road' sign and take this track, keeping the cliffs of Nyangani up to the left, and passing the remains of an ancient fort on a hill on the right, to reach Nyazengu Campsite after about one hour.

(You can stay at Nyazengu Campsite for two nights and take their marked hiking trail up a valley called Tucker's Gap onto the southern side of Mount Nyangani. This takes all day, and more information is available from the park HQ.)

From Nyazengu Campsite, continue following the track, to fork right at a junction and follow a ridge between two valleys. About one hour from the campsite you pass a sign marking the boundary of the Nyazengu Nature Reserve and then a No Entry sign, referring to vehicles coming the other way, where a faint track to the right drops down to the river. Beyond the river remnants of terracing can be seen.

Keep to the main track, ignoring another faint track on the right (used by fishermen). About four hours from the campsite you reach a spectacular viewpoint on the left overlooking the Pungwe Gorge. Far below you can see the steepsided canyon with the Pungwe River flowing over rapids and waterfalls.

From this viewpoint, follow the track steeply downhill, taking a sharp turn right, to reach a track joining from the left. (This leads to the top of Pungwe Falls, reached after 15 minutes.) Continue on the main track to reach Pungwe Drift, about 4½ hours from the campsite.

Near Pungwe Drift are two national park cottages. You can stay here (if you make a reservation in advance at the park HQ) but camping is not officially allowed. If you stay here for two nights, you can explore the surrounding area, visiting Pungwe View (5km), which overlooks the Pungwe Falls from the south (i.e. the other side of the river to the track from Nyazengu), and the spectacular M'tarazi Falls (14km), the highest waterfall in Zimbabwe, in its own separate national park.

If the park cottages are not available, some of the farmhouses in the area offer accommodation. The most reasonably priced is Brackenridge Farm, on the left side of the Brackenridge Road (directions below), about 5km from Pungwe Drift, where a self-catering cottage is available for about Z$50 per person. Reservations may be required at weekends and holidays, either direct to Mr Jackson, PO Box 6, Juliasdale, Tel 129 26312, or through the Tourist Office in Mutare.

From Pungwe Drift, it is a pleasant 14km walk on tracks through farmland, plantation and natural woodland to the main Mutare - Nyanga road. From the drift, walk up the hill, to fork left at a junction, then right after 2.5km onto Brackenridge Road (straight on leads to Pungwe View and M'tarazi Falls) and follow this to meet the main road after about three to four hours. From here, you can wait for a bus or hitch back to Mutare or Nyanga.

Connemara Lakes, World's View and Eagle's View

To the north of the national park, near the village of Troutbeck, are the picturesque Connemara Lakes. A few hundred metres from the lakes is the western edge of the Nyanga Range, where the land drops sharply, over 1000m, down to the plains below. The appropriately named World's View is on the escarpment edge. Eagle's View, on a rocky spur about 2km to the south, offers an even more spectacular panorama.

Several short hikes are possible in this area. From Nyangombe you can hitch quite easily, or wait for the daily bus, to Troutbeck where a track turns left off the tarred road and climbs up through plantation to reach World's View (7km, about two hours' walk).

From World's View, you can scramble up the rocky ridge to the north of the viewpoint. On the summit are the remains of a pre-colonial fort. Views down the dramatic escarpment edge contrast with those over the gentle-looking Connemara Lakes, surrounded by private houses, with manicured gardens running down to the side of the lake.

To reach Eagle's View, follow the main track southwards back towards Troutbeck. After 700m an old track, closed to traffic, branches off to the right keeping close to the escarpment edge. Eagle's View can be seen to the right about 1km from the start of the closed track. The views from this point are better than those at World's View but fewer people come here because you can't drive all the way! To regain the main track, continue on the old track, branching left at the first junction.

Nyangombe Falls

The walk to the falls, past Udu Dam, is undulating and not too interesting, but the falls themselves (about 30m high) are beautiful and well worth a visit. To get there from Nyangombe Campsite, cross the main tarred road and follow the signposted track for about 6km to reach the falls.

Paul Hunt sent us the following information about his hiking routes in the Nyanga National Park:

Another worthwhile short hike is from the panoramic World's View down the steep slope to Nyanga. I managed to hitch up to Troutbeck from where I walked up the track to World's View. Directly down the slope is a narrow path which descends into the valley and leads to the dirt road to Inyanga. From Nyanga village it's possible to hitch or walk back to the campsite.

The area between the campsite and Nyangani Mountain is littered with ruins of previous settlements including stone forts on hill tops, pit structures, and terraced hillsides. Although camping is not officially allowed I camped in the valley below the mountain. Next day I followed the track southwards at the base of the mountain to Pungwe Falls. I met no-one on this trail through what is by far the best scenery in the park. I camped above Pungwe Falls, and next day hiked along tracks to Mtarazi Falls above the Honde Valley. There is a trail leading down into the Honde Valley but it is very overgrown, so I took the forestry roads for about 23km to the main road between Nyanga town and Mutare. The week I spent hiking in Nyanga National Park was very enjoyable and I met few other hikers on the trails away from the holiday lodge areas.

Chimanimani National Park

The Chimanimani Mountains are at the southern end of the Eastern Highlands, the range that marks Zimbabwe's eastern border with Mozambique. They differ from the Nyanga Mountains both geologically and in appearance: whereas the mountains of Nyanga are generally rounded, with few cliffs or exposed rocky peaks, and covered in grass and bush, the Chimanimanis are steeper and more rugged with sharp peaks and ridges, dissected by narrow valleys. The stark grey rock of the Chimanimanis can be seen from many miles away and is particularly dramatic in the evening, when it catches the light of the setting sun and appears to shine white or pink.

The border between Zimbabwe and Mozambique runs right through the Chimanimanis and the eastern part of the range, in Mozambique territory, cannot be reached by tourists. However, the western side of the range contains some of the most spectacular mountain scenery in Zimbabwe and is a 'must' for any hiker.

The name of the range is derived from the local word *T'shimanimani*, which means 'squeezed', referring to the narrow Musapa Gorge, to the north of the range and outside the park. The original name for the range was Mawenje and older local people still use this word.

The entire range on the Zimbabwe side is contained within the Chimanimani National Park but, unlike the Nyanga, this park does not contain lodges, tracks, or even signposts. It is very much a

Chimanimani National Park

wilderness area, and the only way to reach the mountains is on foot. Walking in the Chimanimani range is a more serious undertaking than any of the other areas described in this chapter, but it is also the most rewarding.

Getting there

Chimanimani town (formerly Melsetter) is the nearest settlement to the national park. You can get here from Mutare by car or bus or, with more determination, by hitching. There's also a minibus service between Mutare and the Basecamp, via Chimanimani, three times per week in each direction. It costs Z$50 for the whole trip, or Z$20 for Chimanimani town to the Basecamp. For more details ask at the Information Bureau in Mutare or at the Chimanimani Hotel, or phone Eastern Tours on Chimanimani (126) 294.

To reach Mutekeswani Park Gate (the only official entrance, and the Basecamp campsite) from Chimanimani town take the dirt road opposite the hotel (signposted). After 4km fork left. After a further 6km, at Charleswood, turn left then fork immediately right and then left after 200m. Continue for just over 3km to reach a fork (left goes to the Outward Bound School), keep right to reach the national park entrance and Mutekeswani Basecamp after 2.5km. This total distance from Chimanimani town to the Basecamp is 17km, on driveable track, passing through pine and coffee plantations. If you're walking you should allow about four hours. An irregular bus from Chimanimani town to Mountain Forest village covers the first 10km of this distance, as far as Charleswood.

Places to stay

In Chimanimani town, the comfortable **Chimanimani Hotel** has rooms from around Z$150, and allows camping in the hotel grounds for a small fee. Most travellers stay at **Heaven Lodge** (*a wonderful place to crash out before and after being in the mountains*, Kate Worster), where rooms start at Z$30. Another place is the friendly **Frog and Fern**, which costs Z$85 per person for bed & breakfast, about 2km out of town on the Bridal Veil Falls road.

At the Mutekeswani Basecamp, camping costs Z$20. The site has clean water, hot showers, toilets and fireplaces.

On the mountain range itself is the Mountain Hut which offers simple but perfectly adequate accommodation for Z$60 per night. The hut is in good condition and has basic furniture, beds with

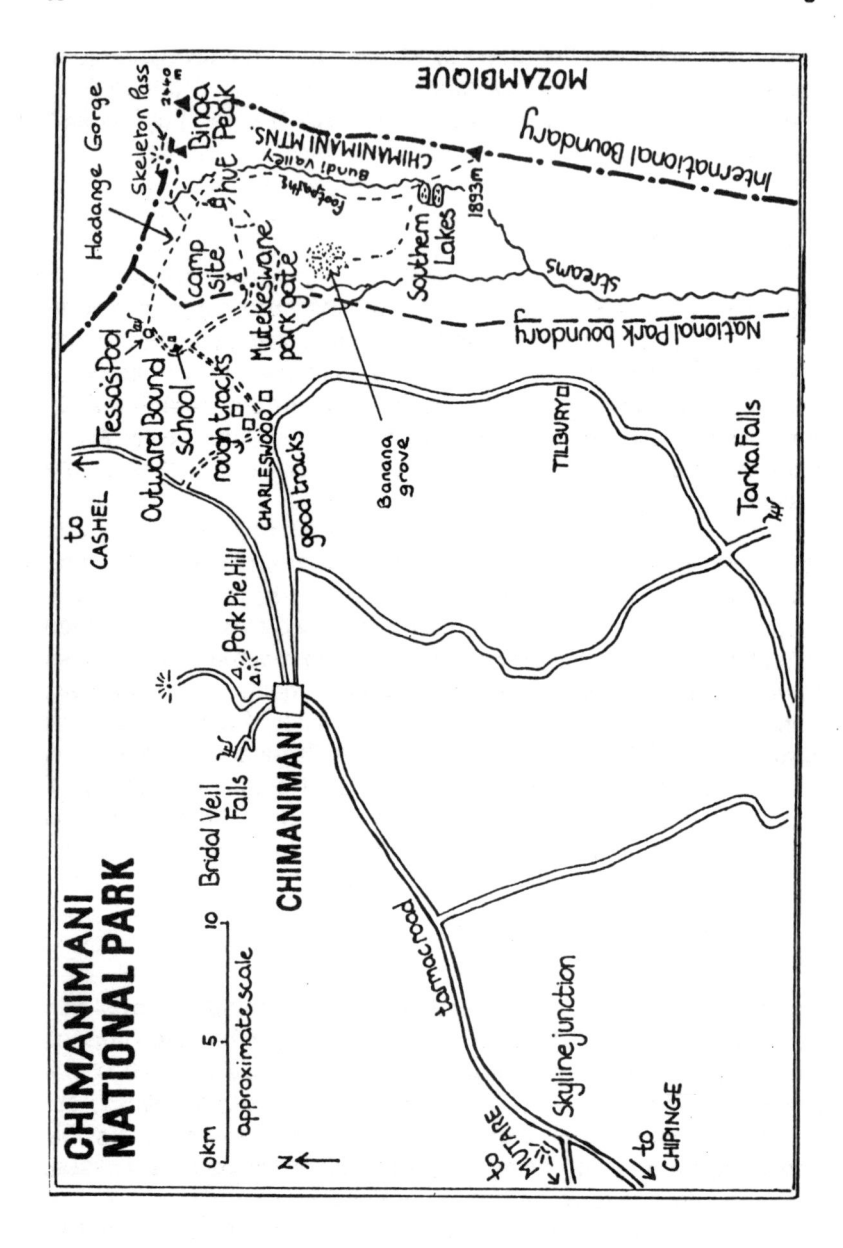

Hiking

CHIMANIMANI NATIONAL PARK

Chimanimani National Park

mattresses (own sleeping bag required), a kitchen with small gas stoves, clean toilets, cold showers and a caretaker. To conserve wood, fires are not allowed in the hut, so it can be cold at night. You need to bring all your own food and cooking gear, plus candles.

Camping is permitted anywhere in the park. Suitable places are mentioned in the route descriptions. We've heard from several travellers who have slept in some of the many caves which dot the mountains. Most caves have informal names, as used by students from the Outward Bound School. Some are easy to find, others are hidden. The park rangers at the Basecamp or the Mountain Hut can advise.

All fees for camping, hut and park entrance are payable at the Basecamp office. Entrance fees are currently Z$20 for visits of less than one day and Z$40 for up to seven days.

Getting organised

For supplies, Chimanimani town has some small shops and a market. Stock up here or in Mutare before going into the mountains. There are no shops in the park. Once you leave the Basecamp, you need to be completely self contained. Paths are not always clear and a compass is recommended.

There is no good quality tourist map of the Chimanimanis, but the Tourist Office in Mutare may have maps of the park which are adequate. Survey maps are available from the map office in Harare. The rangers at the Basecamp may lend you their map, which is tatty and dated, but better than nothing.

If you don't want to walk alone, Howard Barnes Trails organises walking safaris in the Eastern Highlands. For details see the Nyanga section.

Warning The eastern boundary of Chimanimani National Park is also the international border between Zimbabwe and Mozambique. It is illegal to cross into Mozambique. In the past, Mozambique anti-government rebels crossed into Zimbabwe on several occasions and attacked the populated region south of the Chimanimanis. Now Mozambique is at peace it is very unlikely there is any danger; staff at the hotel or national park office in Chimanimani town, or at the park entrance, will advise you if there is.

HIKING ROUTES

The various hiking routes described here can be followed separately, or several can be linked together to form a longer trek including many of the range's most interesting features.

Mutekeswani Basecamp to Mountain Hut

From the Basecamp the path (known as Bailey's Folly) is generally clear and marked by cairns, as it climbs steeply up the first main escarpment of the range, passing through a grassy area where the gradient eases, then through an area of standing buttresses and scattered boulders, dropping slightly past a cairn where a path joins from the right, then dropping again to reach the hut, about two to three hours from the Basecamp.

Mountain Hut to Binga Summit

The hut overlooks the broad grassy head of the Bundi Valley. Binga is the mountain directly opposite the front of the hut, on the other side of the valley. From the front of the hut the path drops steeply through a patch of small trees and divides a few times. Aim directly towards Binga. The path crosses the Bundi stream and winds gradually upwards, then steeply up a small valley, to the crest of a ridge. The path is clear and well cairned as it crosses a flat grassy area, then a stream, and starts climbing again.

About 1½ hours from the hut, at the end of another flat area the path divides; ignore the right fork, which is faint and badly defined, and keep on the main path as it starts to climb the main peak. At a fork keep left, following the cairns, and scramble under a large boulder. Continue following the path to reach a pile of large boulders which have to be scrambled over to reach the summit marked by a concrete bollard. The total time from the hut to the summit is about three hours. Allow the same for the return. (This route should not be attempted in misty conditions.)

Mountain Hut to Skeleton Pass

Take the path that drops steeply through the trees at the front of the hut to fork almost immediately left and follow the clear path across the flat grassy area at the head of the Bundi Valley. The path divides again; keep right (the left leads to the the col above Hadange Gorge) to cross the main stream and continue through grass to cross another stream and turn right to follow the clear path as it climbs steeply up a small valley to reach Skeleton Pass, about one to two hours from the hut. A sign marks the international boundary. From the pass you can see across the Nimozi Valley to the steep sides of Nhamedema Mountain in Mozambique.

From Skeleton Pass you can return to the hut, or go to the col above Hadange Gorge by retracing part of the route down to the bottom of the small valley, but instead of crossing the stream keep it to the left. Follow this path (up to the right are low cliffs and steep grassy slopes), to meet another path coming from the hut. Keep straight on to reach a low point in the skyline, which is the col above Hadange Gorge. From this point you get excellent views down into the gorge and out to the flatter plantations to the west of the Chimanimanis.

You can return to the hut from here or, if descending to the Basecamp, take the route described below, which is exposed and exhilarating but very steep and should not be attempted in wet conditions.

Mountain Hut to Basecamp, via Hadange Gorge

From the hut follow the directions above to cross the head of the Bundi Valley to reach the col above Hadange Gorge. Take the clear path as it descends very steeply through grass and light bush to enter a densely vegetated valley. The path crosses the main stream, then a tributary, and then divides. Fork left, back across the main stream, and continue to follow the clear path down the gorge, with steep grey cliffs up to the left, crossing the main stream twice more, to reach two parallel firebreaks and a fence marking the park boundary, about two to three hours from the col.

From here you can get back to the Basecamp by following the firebreaks, but this is not recommended as they climb and drop steeply several times, gaining and losing height unnecessarily. Instead, continue downhill on the clear path to reach the track which leads to the Outward Bound School. Turn left onto the track and follow it to a junction with the main track coming in from Chimanimani town. Turn left and follow the dirt road for 2.5km to reach the Basecamp. (About one hour from the park boundary back to the Basecamp.)

Diversion to Tessa's Pool After coming down the Hadange Gorge, on meeting the track to the Outward Bound School, turn right, cross the main stream, enter the school gates, and just before the track climbs steeply to the school buildings, take the footpath on the left and follow it to reach Tessa's Pool and waterfall, a picturesque spot where swimming is possible, ideal for cooling off after a hot walk in the mountains. (An extra 20 minutes walk each way.)

Mountain Hut to Basecamp, via Southern Lakes

The Southern Lakes are a group of large pools in the Bundi River, some 8km downstream from the hut. The river flows in an almost straight line down the valley between two large ridges and this route runs close to the river as far as the lakes, then follows the top of the ridge on the east of the valley, before descending to the Basecamp. This is a long route (more than 20km, about eight hours of walking), which can be split over two days if you prefer, camping at the Southern Lakes.

Follow the path that drops steeply from the front of the hut, forking right twice, down to follow the clear path over a small stream, up slightly, and then down again steeply into a tributary valley to reach the foot of the Digby Falls after half an hour.

Follow the clear path down the valley, keeping the river to the left, to reach Peterhouse Cave, a broad overhang (providing reasonable shelter, if the wind is not from the southeast). The path turns sharp right before the cave and climbs above and behind it, meeting another path coming in from the right. Keep left and follow the clear path down the valley, above and to the right of the Bundi River, through open rolling grassland and patches of bush.

About three hours from the hut, the path drops to a group of small pools (camping possible) and crosses a tributary stream by a large boulder. A path joins from the right, but keep straight on. The path continues to follow the main stream then climbs steeply out of the valley and divides (marked by a very small cairn which may disappear); keep left, near the river, and follow the path over some minor tributaries and along a narrow flood plain until it crosses over large boulders. The river and path take a definite bend to the right and the river flows into a large pool with steep-sided banks. This is the first of the Southern Lakes (the others are further downstream in the steepsided valley); a good place to rest, eat, swim or camp for the night. (Four hours from the hut.)

From the Southern Lakes, the path (marked by a cairn) aims west then north back towards the Basecamp. (Ignore the path which crosses the stream and leads up the steep bank opposite, towards Mozambique territory). The path follows the crest of a broad ridge to

Chimanimani National Park

reach a wide saddle between two jagged rock outcrops and pass through an area of standing stones, rock needles and small eroded buttresses.

Beyond this rocky area the path divides. (Right leads back to the Mountain Hut.) Keep left on the ridgecrest to enter the 'Banana Grove', a clump of broad-leafed trees. The path passes through another area of rocks and then another 'banana grove', divides and rejoins, and then crosses over to the left (west) side of the ridge to drop steeply down the escarpment. At certain times of year the grass here becomes very long and the path difficult to follow, especially as it passes through several densely vegetated valleys containing boggy streams, but it continues to drop, turning left at a large stream and following this downhill to leave the vegetation and reach a firebreak. (Three hours from the Southern Lakes.) A nearby sign warns visitors not to collect plants or firewood.

Cross the firebreak and follow the narrow path to reach a second firebreak and fence marking the park boundary. Go through a gate, turn left and follow the firebreak for 20m. The path is on the right and continues downhill to cross two streams and become indistinct. Continue uphill through light woodland to meet an old track running north-south along the valley side. Turn right onto the old track and follow it to meet the main track from Chimanimani town to the Basecamp. Turn right onto this track to reach the Basecamp (45 minutes from the firebreak).

Easy options

If you don't manage to make it up into the mountains, there are a few places to see which can be more easily reached from Chimanimani town. These are Bridal Veil Falls, a picturesque waterfall about 5km from the town, and Pork Pie Hill, 7km from the town from where sunrise and sunset on the main range can be spectacularly viewed. There is also an Eland Sanctuary near the town: ask at the hotel for details.

Thanks to Paul Hunt (Britain) and Jenny Mothoneos (Australia) for their hiking information, incorporated into this section.

Mavuradonha Wilderness Area

The Mavuradonha Mountains are in the north of Zimbabwe, close to the border with Mozambique, where the central plateau of the highveld gives way to the broad Zambezi Valley. The southern slopes of this range form one of the steepest sections of the Zambezi Escarpment, over 600m high, where rolling fertile farmland changes suddenly to dry flat bush-country.

The mountain range has been incorporated into the Mavuradonha Wilderness Area, which was established to protect this area from settlement or cultivation. A wilderness area, unlike a national park, is administered by a local council and the income generated by the area goes directly to the local people, in the form of schools, clinics and other community facilities, rather than into the national treasury. Mavuradonha Wilderness Area was gazetted in 1988 and is administered by a committee consisting of councilors from Mzarabani District Council and local farmers and ranchers.

Mavuradonha is complete wilderness; totally unspoilt and undeveloped. There are no roads and only a few footpaths. Visitors are encouraged to walk where they please, through the dense woodland or across open grassy plateaux, to reach the edge of the escarpment and enjoy the spectacular views over the Zambezi Valley. Guides can be provided but are not obligatory, and camping is permitted anywhere.

Walking in Mavuradonha is a unique experience and a wilderness area of this type is still a new concept in Zimbabwe, and very much an experiment in practical conservation which deserves support. The founders of Mavuradonha Wilderness Area, the Ministry of Natural Resources and the Government of Zimbabwe should be congratulated for their efforts to conserve this area for the benefit of the people of Zimbabwe, as well as for hikers and all visitors to the country.

Getting there

The nearest town to Mavuradonha is Centenary, reached from Harare via Mazoe and Mvurwi. It is possible to hitch. From Centenary, keep on the tarred road towards Mzarabani and Msenbezi. Pass through Mavuradonna village, to reach a track on the right signposted Mavuradonha Wilderness Area. This point is 50km from Centenary (marked by kilometre pegs at the side of the road). The area HQ and campsite are 200m down the track. Total distance from Harare, 197km.

Mavuradonha Wilderness Area

Alternatively, a daily bus runs between Harare and Msenbezi. After Centenary, look out for the kilometre posts and warn the driver in good time that you want to get off at the bus stop about 1km past the track to Mavuradonha Wilderness Area.

Places to stay

There is a campsite, simple huts and plans to build a more comfortable lodge. More information is available from Mr Chris Pohl, Mavuradonha Wilderness Area, PO Box 30, Centenary, or from Safari Interlink Tour Agency in Harare.

Getting organised

Supplies are available from Centenary, but if you're coming on the bus it may be better to load up in Harare.

There is no tourist map of the area, but the central part of Mavuradonha, including the area around the HQ, is shown on the official survey map (1:50,000) number 1631 A3. This map is dated, and some items shown, such as roads and settlements, have changed but topographical detail remains the same.

Hiking routes

Several paths have been cut through the bush in the area around the HQ. Walks can take between two and six hours and visit interesting local features such as the Sohwe Falls, the bamboo forest or the summit of Banirembizi, the highest peak in the range (1622m) which gives excellent views over the flat plains of the Zambezi Valley to the north and the farmland around the Muzengezi Valley to the south. Paths are re-cut differently each season. The staff at the HQ will tell you which paths are open.

Apart from these cut paths, which cover only a small portion of the area, Mavuradonha remains totally undeveloped wilderness which, for keen hikers, is its very attraction. Visitors are encouraged to explore the area on their own. Guides can be provided on request, although advance notice is usually required. You need to be completely self-contained. From April to August a tent is not usually necessary as the nights are generally warm and dry, although a mosquito net is recommended. Sleeping out under the stars, surrounded by the sounds of the African night, is one of the best ways to experience the wilderness.

Hiking

THE TRAVEL BOOKSHOP

A TREASURE CHEST FOR ALL TRAVELLERS

"The Travel Bookshop has never failed me in any quest for a book in any form about travel or place. Literature, guide books, humdrum travelogues... it has stocked them all, both newly published and long out of print. It was the first shop to specialise in this topic and it has remained unquestionably the best." GEOFFREY MOORHOUSE

13 BLENHEIM CRESCENT LONDON W11 2EE
TEL: 071-229 5260 FAX: 071-243 1552

Chapter Four

Places of Interest

In this chapter I describe briefly a selection of places of interest that can more easily be reached by independent travellers. Of course, Zimbabwe has many other places which are worth visiting, if you've got the time, money and mode of transport required, but for reasons of space they cannot be included in this chapter. If you need more details about a specific place not mentioned here, you can normally get the information from a tour agent in Harare, or from one of the tourist offices or publicity bureaux listed in the *Cities and Towns* chapter.

Bvumba Mountain

Bvumba Mountain (formerly Vumba Mountain) lies about 30km to the east of Mutare, at the centre of the Eastern Highlands. On the mountain are the Bunga Forest Reserve and the Bvumba Botanical Reserve, established to protect indigenous forest species, and the Vumba Botanical Garden, an immaculately displayed collection of endemic and exotic flowers. The small reserves and the garden contain networks of well-marked footpaths where visitors can wander at will. Long-distance hiking is not possible on Bvumba; the area is more suited to gentle rambling, particularly for birdwatchers and walkers with an interest in plants and flowers.

Detailed route descriptions are not necessary as the paths through the reserves are all well-marked. Numerous permutations are possible. Information sheets, with accurate sketch maps, are usually available from the warden's office. You should use the maps and explore on your own.

Getting there

From Mutare, there is a bus to Bvumba on Fridays and weekends only, but hitching at other times is not difficult. From the city centre take the main road south (towards Birchenough Bridge) for about 2km, then turn left onto the Bvumba Mountain Road. A short distance up this road is a petrol station - the best place to hitch. From here it's 32km to Bunga Forest and another 2km to Vumba Reserve. The road is tarred all the way.

Places to stay

It is possible to visit Bvumba for the day if you are staying in Mutare (details of accommodation in the *Cities and Towns* chapter). There are also several self-catering cottages on Bvumba mountain (charging from Z$100 per person); the Publicity Bureau in Mutare can provide a full list.

For budget travellers, the undoubted favourite is the **Cloud Castle Guest House**, near the entrance to Vumba Reserve, which has rooms from Z$40 per person. Other luxuries include hot showers, a kitchen for self-catering, a big log fire and shelves full of books. For reservations or more information contact Mr Hancock, PO Box 957, or Tel: Mutare 217620 (evenings).

The Vumba Reserve has a **campsite** with hot water, clean toilets and showers, fireplaces, swimming pool, and an excellent view to the east of the Mozambique plains, for the usual Z$20.

For supplies, it's best to bring what you need from Mutare, although there is a small shop, selling basic items, near the reserve entrance. In the gardens is a tea-room serving drinks, snacks and light meals.

Chinhoyi Caves

On the main road between Harare and the Zimbabwe/Zambia border, some 10km north of Chinhoyi town (formerly Sinoia), large caves, one with a deep blue pool at the bottom, are worth a visit if you're passing. The surrounding area is a national park and entrance fees are payable. There's a small campsite and hotel nearby.

Hwange National Park

Hwange (formerly Wankie) is usually regarded as Zimbabwe's finest game park. You need a car to tour most of the park, but walks and game-drives are organised every day from the park headquarters at Main Camp, where there's a campsite, chalets, shop and restaurant. Usual national park entrance and camping charges are payable here. Many travellers report that once you've got to Main Camp, a car is not at all essential and a visit is enjoyable and rewarding.

Getting there

Without a car, reaching Main Camp is tricky. Buses between Victoria Falls and Bulawayo can drop you at the turn-off into the park, where you might be able to hitch a lift. Trains stop at Dete from where you may also be able to hitch. However, the best way is to get the bus which goes three times per week between Bulawayo and Vic Falls via Safari Lodge, right on the edge of the park, about 20km in towards the park from the main road turn-off. From Safari Lodge to Main Camp you can catch the shuttle bus operated by UTC, or try hitching (which many people do, although technically this is not allowed inside the park).

Alternatively, safaris to Hwange can be arranged in Harare, Bulawayo and Victoria Falls. If you shop around, and get a group together, you can sometimes get a bargain deal.

Mana Pools National Park

Mana Pools National Park is in the north-west of Zimbabwe, between the Zambezi River and Zambezi Escarpment. The park is well maintained, and scenically stunning with an impressive selection of wildlife. Travellers without a vehicle might consider visiting this park as walking is permitted here, although getting *in to* the park without a car can be very hard. The park is only open from May to October, inclusive.

The place to aim for is Nyamepi campsite, 73km from the main road between Makuti and the Zimbabwe-Zambia border. Hitching is difficult as most private cars are already loaded up. The best place to wait for a lift is the park office (where all visitors have to report before entering the park) at Marongora, 16km north of Makuti on the main road. You have to pay your own park entrance and camping fees here. The rangers here may let you camp behind their office if you get stuck. August is the busiest month (school holidays), and the park is closed during the rainy season (November—April).

You can base yourself at the main campsite at Nyamepi, on the banks of the Zambezi, taking short walks from there. Longer walks into the bush are not recommended, and may be forbidden for inexperienced walkers (when new laws are introduced) as close encounters with lion, elephant or buffalo are a distinct possibility. You can arrange to be accompanied by a ranger (who will expect to be paid) or join an organised walking safari.

Chipembere Safaris organise a range of safaris in Mana Pools which combine walking in the bush, canoeing on the Zambezi and wildlife viewing from a Landrover. Their 4-day canoe safari and 4-day backpacking trail are not cheap (US$400) but excellent value and highly recommended. Safaris start from Kariba, at least once per week, and if you're there it's usually possible to arrange things on the spot. Alternatively, book in advance: contact Mr Steve Pope, Chipembere Safaris, PO Box 9, Kariba, Tel 2946, or through Safari Interlink or any travel and tour agency in Harare.

Great Zimbabwe Ruins

The Great Zimbabwe Ruins are described by archaeologists as the the largest and most important pre-colonial stone structure south of the Sahara. For visitors today, it's a fascinating place and highly recommended if you're passing anywhere close.

This 'city', covering several square kilometres and built entirely of cut dry-stone blocks, was contructed between the 12th and 15th Centuries, and was the capital of an African state which covered much of modern-day Zimbabwe and parts of Botswana, Mozambique and South Africa. The name is thought to derive from the Shona words for 'great houses of stone'. It was adopted as the name of the modern country after independence, when the title Rhodesia was dropped.

As the site is a national monument, a small entrance charge is payable. This includes entry to the on-site museum which will give you all the details about the history and archaeology of the site.

There's a campsite right next to the ruins where it's best to stay two nights so that you can explore the ruins fully on the day in between. (Bring all the food you need, though, as there are no shops nearby.)

The Great Zimbabwe Ruins are 30km south-east of Masvingo. There's a bus every morning from the Mucheke suburb of Masvingo, or it's possible to hitch. You can start hitching from Masvingo

Great Zimbabwe Ruins

Publicity Bureau, or cross the river to the Craft Centre, then turn left to Mucheke suburb, and hitch from near the bus station.

Victoria Falls

Most travellers agree that the Victoria Falls are one of the most impressive natural features in Africa. The mile-wide Zambezi River drops 100 metres into a narrow gorge creating enough spray for a lush rain forest to have become established in the immediate area. Its local name is Mosi O Tunya — 'the smoke that thunders' — and it's easy to see how it got this name. The area around the Falls has been declared a national park and standard park charges are payable to enter.

It is possible to view the Falls from just about every angle: from Livingstone's statue looking along the gorge on the Zimbabwean side where the double rainbows are at their best; from right opposite the lip of the Falls on the other side of the gorge (you'll get wet but it's worth it!); from Knife Point on the Zambian side, where you can see a complete circular rainbow when crossing the footbridge; from upriver on a pleasure-boat cruise; and even from above on a 15 minute 'Flight of Angels' plane ride. In the evening look for the lunar rainbow at the falls (it doesn't have to be a full moon).

You can cross to the Zambian side for a few hours with very little fuss. Declare your Zim dollars when leaving; a receipt will be issued and the money returned with no problems when you re-enter.

Getting there

The town of Victoria Falls has grown up around the falls themselves, and is now a major tourist centre, with hotels and a campsite, cafes and restaurants, shops and tour agents. This is the centre for white water rafting, and safaris into Hwange or some of the other national parks in this part of Zimbabwe can be organised here. Victoria Falls is most easily reached from Bulawayo by daily bus or train. Hitching is also possible.

Places to stay

The most popular place for budget travellers, is the **campsite** in the town centre (next to the Tourist Office) with all the usual facilities, including a lock-up room for baggage, for Z$20 per night, per person. The site also has a dormitory for Z$30, and chalets for Z$50 per night, although these are often booked up well in advance. However, there is a good chance of getting a chalet if you go to the park office around 6pm. Any reserved chalets not taken up by then are made available.

Most of the other hotels in Vic Falls are fairly luxurious and beyond the bounds of travellers on a tight budget. But all sorts of buildings are going up in the town and there are rumours of a new 'backpackers' hostel', so make enquiries when you arrive.

For eating in Vic Falls, the near-legendary Wimpy Bar is eternally popular. Chris and Emma Tatton (Britain) write: *The lunch buffet at the Vic Falls Hotel is very good value — real luxury and great scenery. But they don't like it if you share a plate between two!*

Getting around

The Falls themselves can be easily reached from the campsite in the town (about 2km), and there are several other good day-walks that can be done in the area: along the banks of the Zambezi or up into the hills behind the town. The Tourist Office sometimes has maps of the area.

For exploring further afield, bicycles can be hired in Victoria Falls town (three places). It's possible to use a bike to cross over to the Zambian side of the Falls (via the road bridge) and even go on into the town of Livingstone which is about 10km from from the Zambia customs post.

Rafting

Vic Falls is the centre for Zimbabwe's white-water rafting industry. For travellers in southern Africa, to ride the Zambezi rapids below the falls has become an essential part of the trip. There are raft trips every day, when the water is high enough (during and after the rainy season), with several flotillas of inflatable boats, each carrying six to ten people, making the all-day journey.

You can arrange everything on the spot through one of the rafting companies or tour agents in Vic Falls. Rafting is so popular these days that all boats are sometimes full, but if you wait for a day or two they can normally find you a space. Conversely, sometimes bookings are a bit slack and you can negotiate a cheaper deal, especially if you get a group together.

If you want to find out more, a video of the previous day's rafting exploits is shown in the bar of a hotel in the town centre every night.

Victoria Falls

Staff are on hand to answer any questions. You can even buy a video of your own trip — as, unless your camera is waterproof and indestructable, you won't have any photos!

If your time is limited, you can make a reservation in advance at a tour agent in Harare or even at the airport a few minutes after touching down!

Rafting trips cost between US$70 and US$100, payable in hard currency, which includes training, safety gear, transport, the all-day trip and even your lunch. Not cheap but good value. We have yet to hear from anybody who didn't think it was the experience of a lifetime.

Neil Irving (Britain) sent this account: *White water rafting at Vic Falls is expensive but something out of this world. The run we did was about 10km with twelve rapids, one of which was grade 5 (grade 6 is impossible). You get very wet, very frightened, but it's like nothing else!*

ONE WORLD TOURS

You've whetted your appetite with a Bradt Guide ... now fulfil your dreams with a *One World Tour!*

All our tours respect the culture and environment of the countries we go to and help conserve them.

So for insight, adventure and the holiday of a lifetime in Latin America, Asia and Africa, phone or write for a brochure.

One World Tours Ltd, 80 Stuart Road,
London SW19 8DH
Tel: 081-946 6295 Fax: 081-946 1985

In the north of Chobe Park there are so many elephants there is not enough vegetation to support them. They look very thin and bony - a sad sight.

PART TWO

BOTSWANA

A point to consider...
For independent travellers on a limited budget, Botswana can be problematical: once you leave the main routes, public transport is virtually non-existant and hitching is painfully slow; there is little in the way of cheap accommodation; most food is imported and therefore costly; and, as part of the Botswana government's policy of promoting 'low density, high cost' tourism, entrance fees for the national parks and wildlife reserves are high. Fortunately, the country's main attraction, the Okavango Delta, can be reached and explored by independent travellers, although it is still not cheap. The information provided here reflects this situation and is therefore brief. To see the rest of the country you need your own vehicle, a lot of money, and another book!

BOTSWANA

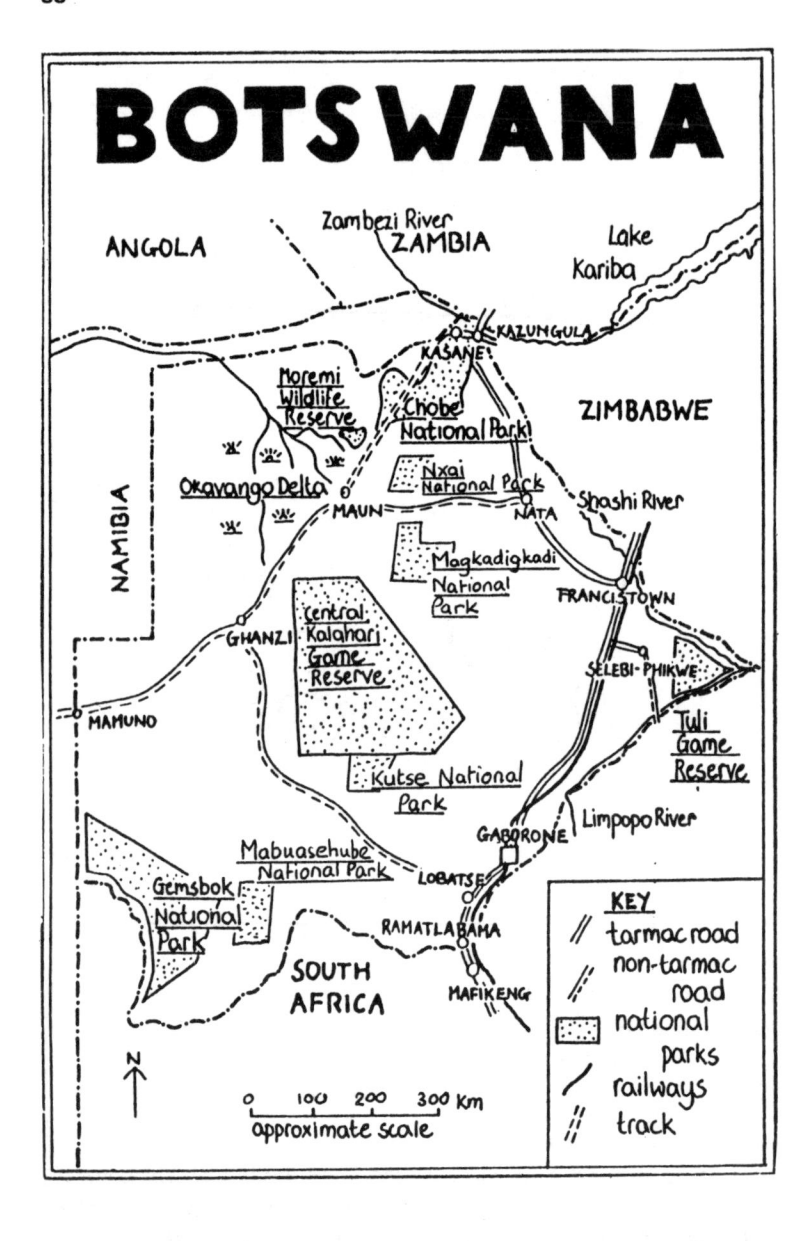

Chapter Five

Facts and Figures

Botswana is a land-locked nation of over 600,000 square kilometres (231,000 square miles) making it almost three times the size of Great Britain. Ninety per cent of the population, of just under one million, is fairly evenly dispersed over the eastern third of the country where there is fertile land with sufficient rainfall for growing crops and raising cattle. At the urban centres around Gaborone, Selebi-Phikwe, Francistown and other large towns, the population is highly concentrated. More than two thirds of Botswana is covered by the great Kalahari Desert and here the population is sparse.

In the dry season (May-September) it is cool with temperatures averaging 25°C. It gets much colder at night and frost is not unknown. In the wet season it gets warmer; temperatures in December and January can reach a humid 40°C. Most rain falls in the eastern regions. There is very little rain in the Kalahari Desert.

Botswana relies heavily on South African co-operation for the development of its economy. Most of the population is involved in agriculture and meat exports account for 30% of Botswana's total export. Other major exports include diamonds, copra-nickel and coal.

People and languages

There are nine separate groups of people ('tribes') in Botswana, the dominant one being the Tswana. Nomadic tribes of San (Bushmen) inhabit the Kalahari Desert region. There are a number of expatriates from Western countries involved in the various mines and industries and living mainly in Gaborone or other towns in the Eastern region.

English is the official national language and is spoken to a certain extent by most people who have attended secondary school but nearly everybody speaks Setswana, the language of the Tswana tribe. Other languages include Sakalaka, which is spoken by the people in the north-east, and several San languages spoken by the Bushmen of the Kalahari (often called the 'click' language.)

History

The original inhabitants of this region were the San (more commonly called Bushmen), one of the oldest races of people in Africa. From the middle of the 15th Century the Tswana people moved into what are now the eastern border-lands gradually pushing the Bushmen further west into the drier desert regions.

With the expansion of the Zulu nation in the 19th Century and, not long afterwards, the arrival of the Afrikaaner trekkers the Tswana changed from being a fairly loose-knit people to a structured and highly organised federation of states. The region became known as Botswana, which means Land of the Tswana.

By the end of the 19th Century, the European powers were claiming territories in the region, during the period known as 'the scramble for Africa'.

In an attempt to keep the route open to other British colonies in central southern Africa, Botswana became a British Protectorate in 1885 and was called Bechuanaland, earning itself the dubious distinction of being the only country in the world whose capital city was outside its own borders, it being administered from Mafikeng in South Africa.

Bechuanaland found it difficult to compete with its prosperous neighbours, South Africa and the Rhodesias, and declined. Most people lived subsistence lifestyles and many of the men migrated to South Africa to work in the mines leaving only a few families who were able to survive and increase their wealth from cattle farming.

Independence was granted in 1966; the new capital was Gaborone, and the country's first president Seretse Kharma, a member of one of the most wealthy cattle-farming families. Although he joined the presidents of other southern African countries in opposing apartheid in South Africa, Seretse Kharma was very much dependent on South Africa for his country's railway system and for the wages his people could earn in the mines.

In 1987 the nine 'front-line' nations which form the Southern African Development Co-ordination Conference managed to attract aid and potential investment commitments from a number of Western nations in an effort to break South Africa's virtual stranglehold on the region.

Coming and going

There are regular flights to Gaborone from London on a range of airlines, although to date there is no non-stop service. Check for special deals at the agents listed in the *Zimbabwe — Coming and going* section.

Coming overland there are a number of border crossing points between Botswana and the neighbouring countries of South Africa, Zambia, Zimbabwe and Namibia.

When crossing into South Africa at Ramatlabama on the Gaborone-Mafikeng road, you actually cross into the 'independent homeland' of Bophuthatswana. The road and railway cross the border here and it's no problem to hitch.

The main crossing points between Botswana and Zimbabwe are at Plumtree/Ramokwebana on the Bulawayo-Francistown road, and at Kazungula in the north, on the Zambezi River to the west of Victoria Falls. Both these border-posts are normally fairly hassle-free to cross in either direction.

The border between Botswana and Zambia is also at Kazungula where a large ferry crosses the Zambezi River. The ferry operates every day and is a good place to find a lift in a lorry heading north to Lusaka or even Dar es Salaam, or down to Gaborone or Johannesburg.

There are two 'main' crossing points between Botswana and Namibia: Buitpos/Mamuno on the Windhoek-Maun road is very quiet because the road is bad and there is very little traffic; it is also possible to drive along the Caprivi Strip from Namibia into Zambia briefly and then to cross on the Kazulunga ferry into Botswana, but traffic here is also very light, and you'd need a lot of patience to hitch a lift this way.

Regulations

No visa is necessary for residents of South Africa, the British Commonwealth, U.S.A. and Western European countries for visits up to 90 days.

Currency declaration forms are issued on arrival and must be filled in when changing money. They are checked on departure.

Money

The monetary unit is the Pula (P) which is divided into 100 Thebe (pronounced 'tebay'). At the time of writing the Pula is a fairly stable currency and there is no blackmarket inside Botswana. There is no limit to the amount or type (local or foreign) of money you bring into the country, but you are only allowed to take P20 out. The official bank rate is UK£1 = P3.5 approx, US$1 = P2 approx.

Banks are generally efficient. Visa card customers get their own desk in some banks: useful for drawing cash quickly.

It is interesting to note that 'Pula' is also the Setswana word for 'rain' — a valuable commodity in Botswana.

Transport

Road There are good tarred roads from Kasane and Kazungula in the north, through Francistown and Gaborone, to the border with South Africa at Ramatlabama. The road from Nata to Maun is also tarred, and other sections of road around the country are being continually improved.

Buses run on all the main routes. Hitching is easy. Many local people hitch, but everybody is expected to pay. There are even standardised rates between towns. If you get a lift in a truck or pick-up there will almost certainly be local hitchers on board and you can check the 'fare' with them. Drivers in private saloon cars may not expect payment.

Rail The country's only railway line runs from Bulawayo (Zimbabwe), through Francistown and Gaborone to Mafikeng (South Africa). There are two express trains per week in each direction, and some other, slower, local services.

Accommodation

There are hotels in all the large towns but they tend to be expensive, and out of the tourist areas there are very few campsites. However, if you have a tent once you are clear of the towns you can camp just about anywhere. If you're near a village it would be polite to ask the Chief for permission. Travellers report that in small towns the police are normally quite friendly and may allow you to camp in their compound or even give you a space on the floor inside.

Chapter Six

Cities and Towns

Gaborone

Gaborone (often pronounced 'Khaberoney') is a pleasant compact capital. It was built as a 'new city' in 1964, in the run up to Botswana's independence. It is now reported to be one of the world's fastest growing cities. Most travellers comment on the city's soullessness and spend as little time here as possible.

The main shopping and business area, where you can also find most of the embassies, is called The Mall, right in the centre of the city. (There are other malls, with names, in the suburbs.)

Coming and going

There are trains from Gaborone north to Francistown and south into South Africa at least once a day in each direction. There are also buses, and hitching is possible on the main road. The best hitching point if you're heading north, is in the suburb of Broadhurt, where the main road goes over the railway on a level crossing.

Robert Jackson, a traveller from the USA, writes: *I came to Gaborone from South Africa, but arrived late in the afternoon. There was no cheap place to stay, but the overnight train left for Francistown that evening. So I jumped the train and said goodbye to Gabs!*

Places to stay

Most hotels in Gaborone cater for up-market tourists and business travellers. They tend to be expensive and are often full. The cheapest hotel in the city centre is the **Gaborone Hotel**, near the station, with double rooms at P100. The YWCA hostel near the

Cities and Towns

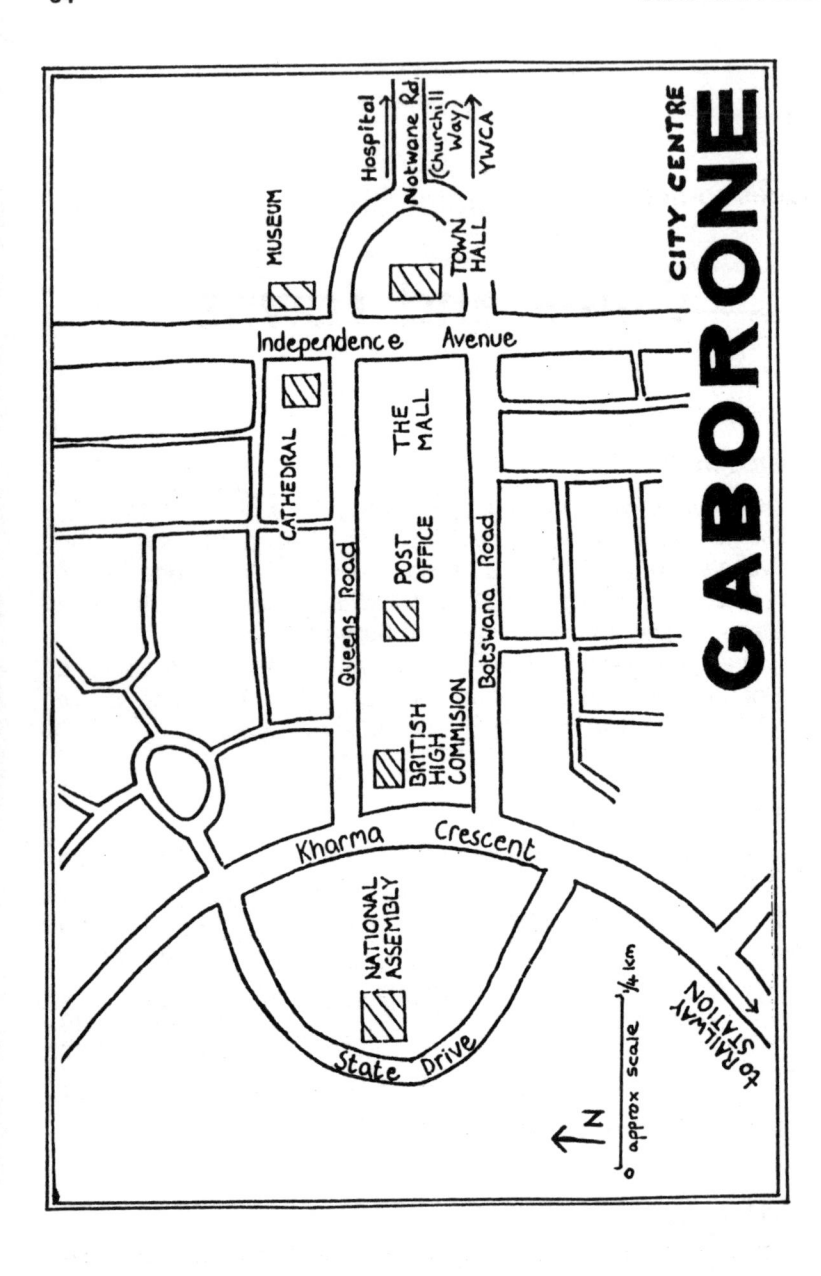

hospital costs P25: it's for women only and, as it's used by local university students, nearly always full. Sleeping at the railway station is said to be OK.

Places to see
If you do have time to spare in Gaborone the **museum** is worth a visit. They have good historical and anthropological displays, and an excellent art gallery. If you want a stroll, go up to the top of Kgali Hill, from where you get a good view of the suburbs.

Francistown
Francistown was originally a 'gold-rush town', and is still surrounded by the remains of abandoned gold-mines. It straddles the junction of the roads from Bulawayo (Zimbabwe), Kazungula, Nata (for Maun and Okavango) and Gaborone, and is more frequented by tourists and travellers than Gaborone.

Coming and going
Francistown is linked to Gaborone and Bulawayo by train and bus. Hitching tends to be quick and easy.

Places to stay
The **Tati Hotel** and the **Grand Hotel**, both in the centre of town charge about P50 per night (double room). Both hotels are a bit run down these days and are fondly referred to by the European 'locals' as "The Grand, which isn't, and The Tati, which is". Favourite for travellers is the campsite at the **Marang Hotel** 5km out of town. The hotel itself is quite expensive, but camping in the pleasant grounds costs P10. If you do arrive late at night, it is possible to sleep at the railway station or the police station for a few hours then walk out of the town in the early morning to start hitching.

Ghanzi
Ghanzi is the self-proclaimed capital of the Khalahari, an inevitable stopover for everyone driving or hitching between Botswana and Namibia. The Kalahari Arms Hotel (the only hotel in town) is expensive but camping is permitted in the grounds.

Kasane

Kasane is a small town, on the Zambezi and the crossroads of the routes between Namibia, Zimbabwe and Botswana. It is also the usual entry point for Chobe National Park. It has shops, a bank and a tourist office. If you're thinking of touring the national park, you can also hire a car here.

Coming and going

Kasane is 10km west of Kazungula (the Zimbabwe-Botswana border). The roads from Victoria Falls and Francistown also converge at Kazungula. Hitching to Vic Falls is usually easy and there's also a daily tourist shuttle bus operated by UTC. Another option for leaving Kasane (particularly if you're short of time) is by air: Mr Roy Ashby of Quicksilver Enterprises has a small plane for hire, and welcomes enquiries from budget travellers. If you get a group of four or five people together this can be a swift, exciting and relatively inexpensive way of getting to Maun (for the Okavango Delta) or anywhere else in the region.

Places to stay

One of the cheapest (and nicest) places to stay is the riverside campsite at **Chobe Safari Lodge**, which costs P12 per person. The hotel has bungalows (starting at P150) and rooms (more expensive), and also arranges bird and animal viewing boat trips on the Zambezi. Campers can also use the hotel swimming pool. Camping and basic accommodation at **Kubu Lodge**, near Kazungula is cheaper but not so good. There is also a public campsite in the park near Chobe Game Lodge (see Chapter Eight, *Chobe National Park*).

Nata

This small town is where the road to Maun leaves the main tarred Francistown-Kazungula road. The bus to Maun stops at the Sua Pan Bar. This is also the best place to start hitching. If you get stuck for the night you can camp behind the noisy Sua Pan Bar (P6) or at the quieter Nata Lodge (15km south of Nata), also P6. There is a post office and bank, open Wednesdays, 10.00-12.00.

Chapter Seven

The Okavango Delta

In the northern Kalahari Desert, northwest of Maun, is the vast watery wilderness of the Okavango Delta. It is formed where the great River Okavango (which rises in the Angolan Mountains to the west) flows into the desert and, quite simply, doesn't flow out again. The river sub-divides into thousands of distributaries, running in narrow channels or lagoons between small islands until eventually all the water evaporates or is absorbed into the soil. The waters rise and fall every year: they are high during the dry season and low during the rains because the flood waters from Angola take five or six months to flow downstream to the Delta.

The Okavango Delta is a huge oasis, and a natural habitat for many species of animals: during the dry season elephant, lion, giraffe, zebra, buffalo, wildebeest, and various members of the gazelle and buck families converge here. Hippos and crocs are permanent residents. Birds are abundant and impressive. These include fish-eagles, saddle-billed storks, cormorants and cranes.

The only way to explore the Delta is by boat: either a traditional wooden dug-out (called a mokoro) or a more modern fibreglass canoe. It is also possible to walk in the Delta by leaving your boat to stroll around some of the islands.

For those on a tight budget, a visit to the Delta can take a major chunk out of the funds, but nearly all the travellers who make it here enthuse about the Okavango's beauty and tranquility and its superb birdlife. This is still one of the most magical places in Africa. To spend a week floating from island to island, camping on a different one each night, is unforgettable.

Tom Edwards from Britain writes: *If you can get there, you MUST go to the Delta. It is a unique place.*

Lars Anderssen (Sweden) writes: *I think you should say that even* though the Okavango is a unique area, visitors will probably not see very much in the way of large mammals. A lot of time, money and hard travelling is required to get to Maun and the Delta, and some travellers get disappointed. They've seen 'Okavango — Jewel of the Kalahari' on TV, and expect an elephant behind every tree.

Getting there

Maun is the hub of the Okavango's tourist industy, and the country's main centre for travellers. The easiest way to reach Maun is from Nata, on the main Francistown - Kasane road. The road is tarred all the way, and you can hitch easily or catch the bus.

Coming from Zimbabwe (Vic Falls-Kazungula) you should first go to Kasane, even if you are heading to Nata, to change money. There is no reliable bank between Kasane, Maun and Francistown, and to get there can take days! (Jurgen Lieb).

If you are a particularly intrepid hitcher it may be possible to get to Maun from Kasane through Chobe National Park. However, there are very few people with vehicles who can give lifts: space is often limited and most who go this way plan a few days safari in the park

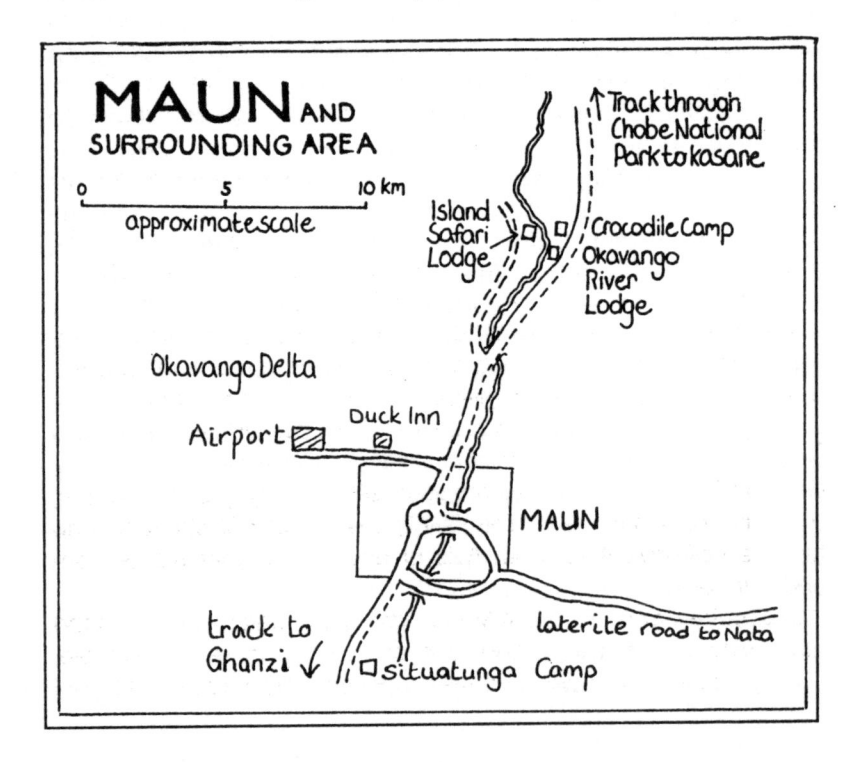

The Okavango Delta

rather than driving straight through (which still takes two days). If you can arrange a lift this way count yourself lucky — and don't forget to take all your food, and enough money to cover the park fees (P60 per day).

It is also possible to reach Maun from Namibia, via Ghanzi to the southwest or via Shakawe to the northwest of the Delta. The hitching here is less difficult but you should still count on a few days for the trip. Both roads in this area are gradually being tarred which may improve things in the future, and at least there are no park fees to worry about if you come this way.

Places to stay

Maun has a real boom town feel about it. Until a few years ago this was due to the growth of tourism in the area, and new camps, travel agents and car hire companies seemed to spring up on a daily basis. Now tourists are outnumbered by civil servants as several government departments have been de-centralised and moved here from Gaborone. The town continues to grow and is changing fast: the streets have been completely reorganised and the airport is being enlarged.

In Maun itself is the famous old **Riley's Hotel**, which started life as a rondavel when Maun was little more than a few rough huts. Today it has been rebuilt, extended and completely modernised and charges P150 for a double room.

Most people stay at one of the camps outside Maun. These have rondavels for around P100 and camping costs P10, and all of them arrange trips into the Delta. Prices vary with the season, so check when you arrive. To reach the camps walk to the edge of town and start hitching, or phone them for a lift (around P35 per person).

Island Safari Lodge (tel: 660300) is about 15km north of the town. This is the biggest camp, with a lively bar and good food, and the best place to meet other travellers. Their mokoro trips into the Delta are popular and usually good value. The Lodge will also hire out a 4WD with driver for trips into Moremi Wildlife Reserve or Chobe National Park. Expect to pay around P280 per day, plus P1 per km, plus fuel, plus park fees. This is expensive but still cheaper than hiring a self-drive 4WD from Avis or one of the other mainstream outfits in town.

Crocodile Camp (tel: 660265) is near Island Safari Lodge, on the other side of the river. Conditions are slightly more comfortable, although reservations for rondavels and camping are preferred, and the food is reported to be excellent (P35 for a 3-course dinner). Trips into the Delta tend to be more expensive but a little less spartan than Island Safari's.

Sitatunga Camp (tel: 660570) is 10km south of Maun on the road towards Lake Ngami and Ghanzi. There is a small shop and bottle-store on the site, a crocodile farm next door, and some nice short walks in the area.

If you arrive in Maun late at night the police are friendly and might let you camp behind the police station at the end of the main street on the right as you go towards the airport. But don't bank on it.

Getting organised

Once you've found a place to stay, you can begin to look around and find a way of exploring the Delta which best suits your budget and timetable. You have two basic choices: either hire a boat near Maun and explore the channels and islands in that region; or fly deeper into the Delta and start from there. The first option is probably cheaper, but the second option is likely to be more rewarding.

Jacqui Green (Britain) writes: *Only at the height of the rains is there sufficient water in the rivers to get into the Delta from the three lodges at Maun. I strongly recommend saving enough money to be able to afford a stay in the interior — it is so much better if you particularly want to see the wildlife, rather than just tick it off your list. Although it is a lot for a budget traveller it was cheap compared with what the average tourist spends, and worth every penny. I don't see the point of going to the Delta and not going into the interior.*

Wherever you hire a boat (fibreglass canoe or traditional wooden mokoro), the price normally includes the cost of a poler/guide to steer the boat and show you the way. This is essential as it's not at all easy to control these boats yourself and very easy indeed to get lost amongst the endless islands and channels of the Delta. Mokoros usually take two people plus luggage and a poler; they are authentic and picturesque but can be uncomfortable. Fibreglass boats usually take three people and are more comfortable. Most poler/guides speak English but this is worth checking beforehand. A lack of communication can be frustrating for both sides and even ruin the trip.

On most mokoro trips aimed at budget travellers you can save money by providing your own food and camping equipment. (On

The Okavango Delta

some trips it's your only choice.) This can be hired from Kalahari Kanvas near the airport, who will rent you anything from a marquee to a knife and fork, or from some camps in the Delta. The poler/guide normally provides his own food and blanket.

Be warned that even if you start in the Delta, you cannot really penetrate the heart of this area if you only give yourself a few days. Some adventurers go out for around 10 to 14 days. As you go north you will notice the ecosystems changing. This makes for a much more interesting trip, although it obviously takes longer and costs more. Having said that, most travellers agree that any time spent in the Delta, however short, is worth it.

Wherever you start from, if you go into the Moremi Wildlife Reserve (the northeastern part of the Delta) you have to pay park fees. Park fees are P40 per day, plus P20 per night for camping. This is high for budget travellers but it does have the overall effect of reducing the number of visitors and therefore the environmental damage in the area while maintaining the government's level of income. (Some travellers argue that their low-budget approach, which requires very little in the way of facilities, is a lot less damaging to the environment than the construction of luxury camps and airstrips.)

Maps and guides

To see where the park boundaries are, or just to see where you're going, maps of the Delta (at a scale of 1:350,000) are available from the Government Survey Office next to Air Botswana. They cost P7.50. For books, there are several general bird and animal field guides available in the shops in Maun. An excellent little booklet called *A Beginners Guide to some Common Trees of the Okavango* has been compiled by Liz Taylor and the polers of Oddballs Camp. You should be able to get it at Oddballs, or by post from Share-net, PO Box 394, Howich 3290, South Africa.

When planning your trip, remember that mosquitoes are prevalent in the Delta and malaria is a risk. Take the usual precautions (see the *Health* section). Also remember that you're going to be in the sun all day: a hat is essential to avoid sunburn or possibly heatstroke.

Exploring the Delta

From Maun In Maun you can arrange to hire a boat from one of the camps outside the town described in the *Places to stay* section.

The camps also seem to prefer catering for groups, and this can make things cheaper, so it's best to team up with some other people if you can. As a rough estimate you can expect to pay around P50 per day for the boat and guide.

Another option for budget travellers is an organisation called **The Swamp Thing**. This outfit is run by the affable Dave and Brett who can be found most afternoons between 3pm and 4pm in the Duck Inn near the airport. Their camp is on the edge of the Delta and can be reached by truck, although the track is very rough. It costs P80 to get there and back, and this fee also covers storage of extra baggage and any administration costs. Mokoro hire is P50 per day. The Swamp Thing has been recommended by several travellers and seems a good option if you're counting every pula.

From inside the Delta In the heart of the Delta are several luxury camps catering mainly for up-market tourists. Most of these places also organise mokoro trips which can be arranged through the various travel agents in Maun. Generally each agent represents one camp, so you need to shop around to compare prices. The camps in the Delta are accessible only by air. Small planes fly out regularly from Maun and a seat costs around P250 return. You can reduce this by getting a group together (more than five) and chartering your own plane. The weight limit for luggage on these flights is usually 10kg per person.

There are two camps inside the Delta which cater for budget travellers. **Oddballs Camp** on Palm Island was the first to specialise in the low-budget market and costs are cheap compared to most of the other camps in the Delta. On top of your flight and park fees, charges are P30 per day for a mokoro and P20 per night for camping. There is a small shop selling food at the camp and you can also hire camping equipment. Oddballs insist that you spend your first and last nights at the camp and at least three days out in a mokoro. (The minimum trip worth doing anyway.) This brings the minimum cost of the trip to about P600 per person, plus food. You can get more information from Okavango Tours and Safaris in Maun, or from their offices in London (tel: 081 341 9442), Montreal (tel: 287 1813) and Jo'burg (tel: 789 5549).

The other budget place is **Gunn's Camp** on Ntswi Island. Run by Mike Gunn, this is slightly smaller than Oddballs and slightly more expensive. Transfers from Maun (by plane or boat) cost P110 and all-inclusive accommodation is P290 per person per day. Their mokoro trips cost P175 per person per day which includes food. If

The Okavango Delta

you have your own food and equipment, camping costs P17.50 per night and the mokoro costs P75 per day. More information from Trans-Okavango Safaris in Maun.

Over the Delta Another interesting way to see the Delta is by air. One-hour viewing flights are available which cost around P500 for a five-seater plane. If you're taking a mokoro trip from inside the Delta, you can even arrange for a flight to drop you at one of the camps. If you fill the plane this can work out cheaper than the normal transfer flight, and you spend much longer in the air.

Leaving Maun

After your trip into the Delta, you can either hitch or catch the bus from Maun back to Nata, from where you can go north towards Victoria Falls or south to Francistown and Gaborone.

You can also try hitching north directly from Maun along the track that goes through Chobe National Park to Kasane and Kazungula, although this can take a great deal of patience. and is not cheap (see the Getting There section).

Alternatively, you can try heading southwards. Tom Edwards, from Britain, wrote with details of his unusual journey around the western side of the Delta, and along the Caprivi Strip:

We hitched south from Maun along the road towards Ghanzi, as far as Toteng and then up to Gumare, a large village. From there we continued to Sopopa (which has one small store) and onto Shakawe, a small town with shops, a post office, and several government buildings. Camping is possible at Hippo Lodge or Shakawe Fishing Lodge (around P10) both 15km south of the town. There's very little traffic; waiting for lifts took a great deal of patience. (Note: The Maun-Toteng-Shakawe road is being upgraded, and traffic is likely to increase in the future.)

From Shakawe we hitched north through Mohembo (a government village) across the border (no problems) into Namibia and the Caprivi Strip. A single road runs along the strip to the small town of Katima Mulilo. There's not a lot of traffic — we got the only vehicle that day. From here we dropped down to re-enter Botswana at Ngoma, at the top of Chobe National Park, about 50km from Kasane.

Hitching to Vic Falls was difficult: most of the vehicles were full. It may be quicker to cross the river at Kazungula and hitch to Livingstone (in Zambia) and than go down to Vic Falls from there. There is a bus from Kasane to Vic Falls every evening (Z$10).

We've seen lots of game, loads of birds, hundreds of logs & shadows but NOT ONE Hippo or Croc!
DON'T DO THAT!! We'll become inundated with them..!
jb

Chapter Eight

Places of Interest

Botswana's National Parks and wildlife Reserves are all very difficult to visit unless you've got your own well-equipped four-wheel drive vehicle. Four-wheel-drive vehicles can be hired in Francistown, Maun and Kasane, but this is beyond the range of most budget travellers. If you do decide to hire a car, when budgeting for the trip remember to include entrance and camping fees, currently P40 and P20 per person per day in national parks, and slightly less in the wildlife reserves.

As an alternative to car hire, several of the safari companies based in Maun and Kasane organise reasonably priced trips into Chobe and/or Moremi. If you shop around and get a group together you may find a bargain.

Some brief details on the two most popular wildlife areas are included here.

Moremi Wildlife Reserve

The Moremi Wildlife Reserve borders the northeastern edge of the Okavango Delta, with a varied landscape supporting a broad range of animals. The southern part of the reserve covers swampland and lagoon and can be reached only by canoe from the Okavango camps, but the northern section covers an area of dry ground and can reached by vehicle. The entrance gate is off the Maun - Kasane road about 160km north of Maun.

There are several public campsites: the one at Third Bridge is particularly recommended. There are no facilities but the setting is perfect for early morning game viewing.

Chobe National Park

Chobe National Park lies in the far north of Botswana, in between Moremi and the Zambezi River. This is Botswana's best game park, and reputed to be one of the best in Africa. It is particularly famous for its great herds of elephant, but the park also contains many other species.

The main entrance into the park is at Kasane (see Chapter Seven), where there are hotels and campsites. Inside the park are several campsites: Serondela can be most easily reached and tends to be often crowded; Savuti is the most popular, near the Savuti Marsh which is an excellent game-viewing area.

Jacqui Green (Britain) writes: *Chobe was an unexpected delight and relatively tourist-free compared with other places like East Africa. I can't recommend it highly enough. However, the campsites are a disgrace with little or no maintenance (Savuti Camp had no water when I was there). Also an elephant had to be shot because tourists had fed it until it became aggressive. It is nice to see animals at such close range, but you can so easily do so anyway in this park so please NEVER FEED THE ANIMALS.*

To keep animals away it's a good idea to keep an electric light on or keep the fire burning all night. Animals naturally stay clear of people and may only come to scavenge. Never bury used cans of food; keep them in the vehicle and dispose of them properly when you get to a town. Never keep any fresh food or anything which may attract animals inside your tent. Check with wardens or other tourists if any rogue animals have been reported in the area.

Luc Lebeau (Belgium) sent us some information about travelling in Botswana and ended by saying: *Please, insist in your book to say that people who really love Africa will be happy in Chobe. OK, the park is very expensive, but for us it's one of the most wonderful parks we have ever seen. It's difficult to find a place where the feeling of nature is so strong, and so nice in infinite calm and serenity.*

PART THREE

GENERAL INFORMATION

Are you **suffering** from *Wanderlust*?

then subscribe to the only magazine that guarantees **no cure**!
Wanderlust is *the* magazine for the independent-minded traveller, covering destinations near and far, plus features on health, news, food, horror tales and eco-tourism, as well as offers, competitions and a hell of a lot more.

Phone or FAX Wanderlust Magazine for special subscription deals on (0753) 620426, or write to Wanderlust, PO Box 1832, Windsor, Berks. SL4 5YG, U.K.

THE GLOBETROTTERS CLUB

An international club which aims to share information on adventurous budget travel through monthly meetings and *Globe* magazine. Published every two months, *Globe* offers a wealth of information from reports of members' latest adventures to travel bargains and tips, plus the invaluable 'Mutual Aid' column where members can swap a house, sell a camper, find a travel companion or offer information on unusual places or hospitality to visiting members. London meetings are held monthly (Saturdays) and focus on a particular country or continent with illustrated talks.

Enquiries to: Globetrotters Club, BCM/Roving, London WC1N 3XX.

Chapter Nine

Health and Security

Before you go

Before going to Zimbabwe and Botswana, check with your doctor about vaccinations you require. These will probably be for Yellow Fever, Typhoid, Meningitis, Tetanus and Hepatitis. (You will also need pills for Malaria.) Plan ahead, as you can't get all these jabs at the same time and some have to be given in series. Contact your nearest Zimbabwe embassy to check which vaccinations are required. Your doctor will also supply certificates. You might be asked to show these certificates when you enter either Zimbabwe or Botswana or any other African country that you may be travelling through.

More advice and information on illnesses and health while travelling in Zimbabwe and Botswana is available from the following:

MASTA (Medical Advisory Service for Travellers Abroad),
The Ross Institute of Tropical Medicine,
The London School of Hygiene and Tropical Medicine,
Keppel Street,
London, WC1E 7HT. Tel: 071-631-4408
(MASTA can provide an individually tailored Concise Health Brief with recent and reliable information, for which a fee is charged. Application forms are available from large chemists or direct from MASTA.)

The Hospital for Tropical Diseases,
4 St Pancras Way,
London NW1 0PE. Tel: 071-387 4411.

Liverpool School of Tropical Medicine,
Pembroke Place,
Liverpool, L3 5QA. Tel: 051-708 9393

Trailfinders Immunisation Centre,
194 Kensington High Street,
London W8 7RG. Tel: 071-938 3939

Thomas Cook Vaccination Centre,
45 Berkeley Street,
London W1A 1EB. Tel: 071-499 4000

In the UK, the MASTA and British Airways jointly operate a chain of travel clinics to advise about all aspects of health while travelling. For more details and the address of your nearest British Airways Travel Clinic phone 071-831 5333.

Have your teeth checked before you go. Dentists in Africa are few and far between. They also tend to be painful, expensive, or both!

Travel Insurance is a very good idea. A policy to cover emergency medication or treatment, as well as loss or damage, might save you a lot of money in the long run. The ISIS Policy, available from STA travel has been recommended.

Diseases and how to avoid them

The medical advice here is brief and phrased very much in layman's terms. Travellers are advised to refer to a travellers' health manual or consult a doctor or specialist clinic. (Details at the end of this chapter and in *Suggested reading*.)

Although standards of cleanliness and hygiene in Zimbabwe and Botswana are nowhere near as bad as they are in some other countries in Africa, in an unfamiliar climate the traveller can still be susceptible and pick up germs from food and drinks which are the major causes of the dreaded 'travellers tummy-bug'.

Diarrhoea

To reduce the chances of contracting diarrhoea, or a more serious disease, take the following precautions:

Always wash your hands before eating. Try to eat food that is

Health and Security

freshly cooked. In the cheaper eating-houses beware of re-heated dishes and uncooked vegetables (eg salads). The water in large towns is usually safe to drink, but in rural or mountain areas use a purifying agent or filter.

If you do get any mild stomach or bowel disorders, don't panic and load yourself up with antibiotics. Take a day or two off food (the first six hours are the hungriest!) but keep your liquid intake up. An illness of this type cannot literally be 'starved out', but avoiding food for a short period helps your body combat the disease. Carbon tablets absorb excess liquid naturally.

If travel is essential during an illness of this type, various medicines are available to ease the discomfort, although most of these (eg Lomotil) only slow down intestinal movements rather than cure the disease.

If the condition does not improve after a few days, you may have contracted a more serious disease such as dysentery. If you feel this is likely consult a doctor. Most large towns have a surgery or hospital. Doctors' fees will usually be charged, but most insurance policies cover this.

Other diseases

Bilharzia/Schistosomiasis, is caused by tiny parasitic worms whose eggs hatch in the body of water snails. The worms can enter your body through drinking or bathing in infected water and then lay eggs in your intestine or bladder. These eggs are discharged when you relieve yourself and if this reaches water with the snails in, the whole process starts all over again. There are very few lakes and rivers in Africa which are free of this disease. Usually the deeper, cleaner and faster-flowing the river, the safer it is. Avoid stagnant water with reeds growing in the shallows, or water near towns and villages. Symptoms include an irritating rash which appears about 24 hours after infection and disappears about 48 hours later. Other symptoms appear about a month later. These can include body swelling, fever, blood in urine or faeces, abdominal pain and lethargy. The disease responds well to treatment if caught in the early stages; if you have had a rash during your travels it's worth having a check when you get home.

Malaria is caused by a blood parasite and is spread by the female Anopheles mosquito. There is no injection against malaria; you need to take pills. As the parasite becomes increasingly resistant to chloroquine in certain parts of Africa, so the prophylactic drugs change, and rather than give advice here, which may be out of date by the time you read it, you should telephone the Malaria Reference Laboratory in London (the Ross Institute for Tropical Diseases) at 071-636 7921. A taped message will give you the most up-to-date information.

With malaria, prevention is more important than cure. Take your pills regularly and on time, as instructed, and do everything you can to avoid being bitten in the first place. Wear long-sleeved shirts and long trousers, and socks too (those little blighters seem to love the area around your ankles!) in the evening if there are mosquitoes about, and sleep under a net whenever possible.

Make sure you start your course of pills at least a week before you arrive in the malarial area and take enough for the journey. Although chloroquine-type pills are usually available in pharmacies in Africa, others are harder to come by.

It's important to keep taking the pills for four to six weeks after leaving the malarial region.

If you do get malaria, most of the drugs used as prophylaxis can also be used as a cure for this disease, when taken in larger quantities. However, if you take any anti-malarial drug in this way, it is essential that you keep to the recommended doses: do-it-yourself treatment is only for emergencies. Malaria is a serious disease which can be fatal and should be treated by a doctor if possible.

Sleeping sickness/trypanosomiasis is carried by the tsetse fly and, although it's quite rare and does respond well to treatment, it's worth being aware of its existence. The tsetse fly is about twice as large as a common European housefly and is recognisable by the 'scissor' position of its wings when stationary. It is fairly common in some parts of Zimbabwe and Botswana, particularly in the Okavango Delta. Symptoms include extreme lethargy, fever, abscesses and swelling of the body tissues. If you think you've got this disease see a doctor immediately.

AIDS is a major disease in Africa. According to the London School of Hygiene and Tropical Medicine, Zimbabwe is a 'danger area', along with a number of other East and West African countries, where a high proportion of the population carry the AIDS virus.

A slight risk exists when receiving blood or blood products as part of hospital treatment, although many hospitals now screen blood products. A rather greater risk exists if you need an injection during

Health and Security

the course of your travels, and the needle hasn't been sterilised. AIDS prevention packs are available from large chemists or travel equipment mail-order companies. These contain needles (for injections and stitches) and other items which may be needed in an emergency. Prices vary. Your doctor will advise.

Other health tips

If you think you have something wrong with you, and it hasn't cleared up after a couple of days, don't put off seeking medical advice. Local hospitals are sometimes unhealthy or poorly supplied, but in every town there is at least one doctor in private practice. They charge for consultations, so check the price beforehand, but it's normally worth forking out if it means you are going to be able to enjoy the rest of your trip. Most travel insurance policies cover visits to the doctor like this.

Using antibiotics is a very serious business. Unless you know what you are doing, don't administer these drugs to yourself. Get advice from your doctor before you leave about what to take and when. And if you do start an antibiotic course keep it up right to the end, even if you do seem to be fully cured half-way through.

Keep cuts clean and covered. Flies are attracted to open wounds and can cause infection.

You'll sweat a great deal if it's hot, but might not notice it because the climate is also quite dry in some areas. Keep your salt intake up, but don't over-do it. A liberal sprinkling on each meal should be sufficient. Salt tablets only help if there's no salt in your diet. Usually they just make you want to drink more.

Watch the colour of your urine. If the colour becomes darker than usual or if you are not urinating as often as you do normally then it means you are not drinking enough liquid. Up your intake to avoid dehydration.

Wear a hat if you are exposed to the sun for a long period of time to avoid headaches and possibly sunstroke. This is particularly advisable on long lorry trips if you're sitting on the back, or in the Okavango Delta

Because everything in Africa goes at a slow pace, be prepared for waits on buses, in offices and shops, in fact, just about everywhere. Don't get annoyed. Stay calm and you'll feel much better in yourself.

Don't let all this talk of diseases put you off travelling. Fortunately, only a few people ever get anything more serious than 'the runs'. Think positive and be careful without being paranoid or a hypochondriac.

Have a full medical check-up when you get back, just to be sure you haven't picked up any lingering diseases. And don't forget to keep taking those malaria pills for four to six weeks after your return.

Security

In most parts of Zimbabwe and Botswana (with the exception of Harare) muggings or robberies are very rare. Unless you really go looking for trouble, wilful violence is very unlikely. But this is no reason for complacency. As always, be sensible. Don't flash your money, camera or other valuables around. Keep your camera in an 'old' bag rather than a nice shiny case. Keep papers, documents, and the bulk of your cash in a pouch around your neck or down the front of your trousers, and keep another purse or wallet for day-to-day spending. This also acts as a 'decoy'. Make sure your pockets are deep and secure. If they're not, sew a button or a bit of velcro on. Several makes of outdoor trousers have zipped pockets. These are ideal.

A small padlock on your pack pockets deters a casual thief in a hotel (and can be used in Harare Youth Hostel where lockers are provided). Alternatively, if you think it's OK, give your valuables or gear to the hotel keeper (or camp guard) if you're leaving your room (or tent) for a while. Keep a separate list of serial numbers of your passport, cheques and other documents and valuables for the insurance in case you lose any of it.

Chapter Ten

Things to Take

In your rucksack

A traveller's rucksack is a very personal thing. All travellers have their own advice about what to take or what not to take, but the basic rule of thumb should always be to carry as little as possible; heavy gear soon becomes a burden.

Don't take too many clothes. This is a common mistake. The following should be sufficient for summer travelling in Zimbabwe and Botswana:

Two pairs of long trousers/One pair of trousers and one skirt
Two long-sleeved shirts
One/two teeshirts
One sweatshirt
One pair of shorts
Two pairs socks
Three/four pairs underwear
One pair of running shoes or light boots
One pair sandals/thongs/flip-flops
One light-weight jacket
Sun hat.

If you are in Zimbabwe during the winter (May to September) or plan to visit the mountain regions at any time of the year, extra clothes are advisable. A thick pullover and pair of trousers, a thermal undershirt and pants, and good wind- and water-proof jacket, warm hat and gloves would all make travelling and hiking more comfortable.

The trousers and shorts should be of a light-weight material, preferably cotton or cotton mix. Trousers are recommended for men and women because, as well as being useful for travelling on the tops of lorries, they are essential to keep the mosquitoes off in the evenings if you're in an area where they are found. There are certain times, though, when a skirt is preferable for a woman. For example, if you are invited to stay at somebody's house, or at some other 'formal' occasion.

If you find your clothing is wearing thin from constant use, it's easy to buy teeshirts, socks, underwear and trousers in shops in the large towns or in markets in African townships. The stuff in the markets is cheaper, but of poorer quality.

It's worth bringing clothes that are fairly new. A favourite shirt that you have had for a few years may look good, but a couple of weeks' travelling is like a year's normal use back home.

This applies to the rucksack itself too. Make sure it's strong enough to stand up to the rigours of long rough rides on a lorry or bus roof-rack. Some travellers carry a strong canvas or plastic sack to put their rucksack in. This protects it from being chafed by ropes, stained by oil or otherwise damaged by goats and chickens, which you may find sharing your transport. The sack can double as a ground-sheet.

A rucksack with a frame is better than a kit-bag or holdall, as even if you don't plan to go hiking you may still find yourself doing some walking, but an external frame can be very awkward and is likely to be damaged. A pack with an internal frame is by far the best. A large dustbin-liner plastic bag placed inside will keep water and dust out.

Some travellers survive with little more than their passport and toothbrush; it's very much a matter of personal choice, but here are some other things you may find useful:

Tent Hotels in Zimbabwe and Botswana are generally expensive. Even the budget hotels are dear compared to other African countries. In Zimbabwe, campsites are cheap and provide excellent facilities. If you're planning to go hiking in the mountains in Zimbabwe or canoeing in the Okavango Delta in Botswana, a tent will give you a lot more flexibility. When buying a tent for travelling in Africa, the recommended criteria are to buy the smallest, lightest tent that you can afford which will be comfortable and stand up to the conditions. Remember you may encounter mosquitoes and heavy rain so make sure that it's well ventilated with fine anti-mosquito screening on the door and windows, and that it has a separate fly-sheet. Also remember that you'll be carrying the tent on your back. Go to a good dealer and ask for advice.

Things to Take

Lightweight Mosquito Net Also very highly recommended for exploring the Okavango Delta or if in the lower regions of Zimbabwe during the warm season. As well as keeping the mosquitoes away, it also keeps the flies off in the morning. They are especially attracted to you if you've been sleeping rough for a couple of nights!

Sleeping Bag If you are camping, a sleeping bag is essential. It can get quite cold in the mountains during the winter in Zimbabwe. A two or three season bag should be sufficient. Alternatively, cheap blankets can be bought in the shops and markets.

Sheet Sleeping Bag Maintains modesty if it's too hot for a full sleeping bag, and also saves your sleeping bag from becoming too grubby on the inside.

Towel and toiletries Don't carry too much. Soap, toothpaste and brushes, and disposable razors can easily be bought in towns and markets. Tampons are usually available in pharmacies in large towns.

Light A small torch, headtorch, or slow-burning candle in a jar. Useful when camping, hiking or canoeing away from an electricity supply.

Camera and film It's best to get all the film you need before you leave. Supplies in Zimbabwe are sometimes unreliable. If film is available it's often very expensive. Supplies and prices in Botswana are on a par with Europe.

First Aid Kit Once again, don't carry too much. Most items can be replaced in pharmacies. Useful items are: sticking plasters (band-aids), antiseptic powder and cream, anti-diarrhoea carbon tablets, lip protector stick, mosquito repellant cream, antihistamine cream, paracetamol/aspirin, AIDS-prevention kit, oil of cloves or similar (for toothache), strong suntan lotion or sun barrier cream.

Other useful things to take are: a length of string, elastic, needle and cotton, some strong sticky tape, water bottle, purification agent and/or filter, notebook/diary and pens, Swiss army-type penknife.

Remember to take all the necessary papers and documents; passport, air tickets, insurance policy, vaccination certificates, identity cards, etc.

Keep all your stuff in strong plastic bags inside your pack. They protect everything from travel damage, rain and dust, or often a combination of all three.

In your wallet

Travellers in Zimbabwe and Botswana can get by on spending very little money, or find their reserves disappearing rather quickly. It all depends on your 'standard of living'. When budgeting, take into account your likely method of travel (express bus, local bus or hitching) and accommodation (hotel, chalet or tent), and the extra costs such as museum and national park entrance fees. A visit to the Okavango will probably be your most expensive outlay.

Your upward limit depends on how well you want to live. If you use public transport, camp and only occasionally eat in restaurants, you'll be spending about £10/US$15 per day on average. If you hitch, sleep rough, and always buy your food from shops or markets you can survive on between UK£3-£7/US$5-$10 per day.

Some people enjoy their holidays more than others – why? Often because experience has prepared them for events and situations that can make a holiday extra special or spoil it.

They probably use the new and extensively improved SafariQuip Travel Accessories range.

The SafariQuip Travel Accessories brochure is essential if you are travelling to a destination outside the highly developed 'western' countries and extremely useful if you're not.

SafariQuip's Travel Accessories are 113 products selected to meet the needs of travellers to exciting and new destinations world wide, chosen to create opportunities for greater enjoyment and comfort and equally important to protect you from the things that can go wrong.

With SafariQuip products you can confidently travel the world.

The SafariQuip Travel Accessories Brochure is free...
Get yours now by phoning 0433 620320 or writing to-
Dept. BPT, SafariQuip, The Stones, Castleton, Sheffield S30 2WX, England. Fax: 0433 620061.

Chapter Eleven

Miscellaneous

Be careful when taking photos of local people in Zimbabwe or Botswana. Children normally love to have their picture taken, but their parents might not be so pleased.

Remember that the whole of Southern Africa is potentially volatile. Within Zimbabwe this is particularly so. Be careful if taking photos near bridges, airports, railway stations, army camps, border posts or anything else that could be considered 'strategic'.

Men and women travelling together might find themselves accepted more readily by the people they meet, and find travelling generally less complicated, if they say they are a married couple.

Some officials that you may come across can appear very awkward, petty or over-zealous. This could be a civil servant issuing you with a visa, or a policeman at a border post. Never lose your temper; it won't make any difference and will probably only make things worse. If the official takes a real dislike to you and your behaviour, it might end up with your passport being 'lost' or you being arrested or turned back.

There are many volunteer workers based in various parts of Zimbabwe and Botswana, working as teachers or medics, or involved in other development programmes. In the past there has been some hard feeling caused by travellers imposing themselves on these people expecting, or even demanding, hospitality. Some of these volunteers might be happy to meet travellers who are passing through their town or village. Others, for whatever reason, might prefer not to. Don't be pushy! If you are invited by a volunteer (or anybody, come to that) to stay for a while, don't scrounge. Pay your way or help by contributing to the day to day costs. Or see if you can do anything useful around the house or garden.

The white residents in Zimbabwe and Botswana are normally very friendly and helpful. In country areas, they are often pleased to meet 'new' people and you may be invited to stay. Once invited, you should be sensitive to your hosts' pace of life. If they are busy, keep out of their way and entertain yourself. If they are not busy, and are pleased to have your company, do your best to be entertaining and pleasant. It might be an idea not to launch into a heavy argument about the current political situation unless you feel you know your hosts very well; your views may differ and cause offence. On the other hand discussing the present state of affairs can be very interesting. Keep an open mind and be prepared to listen.

There won't be many opportunities to be helpful as they will almost certainly have servants, but you can always offer to cook one evening, or maybe take them out to dinner (if you're not on a tight budget) or simply play with the children for a while. Don't outstay your welcome. When leaving thank your hosts and later send a couple of cards or a letter telling them about your journey since you left.

The considerate traveller doesn't save much money by accepting hospitality, but has the chance to make new friends and really learn about a country from the inside.

Addresses have a nasty habit of being passed around between travellers in Africa. If you pass on the address of somebody who took a liking to you and was genuinely hospitable, and an unpleasant or parasitic traveller gets hold of it, it could cause a lot of problems and hard feelings. If you do spend some time staying with people, it's best to keep their address to yourself.

The same applies to your own address back home, or that of your friends or parents. Giving out addresses indiscriminately to all and sundry can result in complete strangers turning up on the doorstep claiming to be friends of friends, and if you're not there, it can be doubly embarrassing for those who are.

APPENDIX

Books and maps
There are plenty of books about Zimbabwe and Botswana, so have a look in your library or a good book-shop. Here's a few that other travellers have recommended:

General and background reading
Lake Ngami and The River Okavango by Charles John Andersson. Published 1856-61. Fascinating records of one of the region's first white explorers.

Travels and Researches in Southern Africa by David Livingstone. Published 1857 in London in London and many subsequent reprints. A record of the travels of the continent's most famous missionary and explorer.

Explorations in South-West Africa by Thomas Baines. Published 1864 in London. The travels of the artist who gave his name to the clump of baobab trees south of Nxai National Park, Botswana.

The Rock Paintings of Southern Africa by the Abbé Henri Breuil. Published by Trianon Press Ltd, from 1955-60 in four volumes and distributed through Faber and Faber.

Okavango: Jewel of the Kalahari by Karen Ross. published 1987 by BBC Publications, London. Another one for the coffee-table, with snippets of excellent background information.

Okavango: Sea of Land, Land of Water, P. Johnson and A.Bannister. New Holland. £17.95. A beautiful book of photos.

Botswana: a Brush with the Wild, Paul Augustinus. £43.75. Illustrated by colour paintings, sketches, and photos; records the author's experiences after living in Botswana several years.

Cry of the Kalahari, Mark and Delia Ownes, Collins (1985), Fontana (1986).
A classic book about the experiences of two American scientists who

spent nine years in the wild, studying lions and many other inhabitants of the Kalahari desert.

Great Zimbabwe, Peter Garlake, Thames and Hudson (1973).
Nicely illustrated and informative book about various investigations, past and present, into the history and background of Black Africa's greatest ancient monument.

Journey through Zimbabwe by Mohammed Amin et al, published by Camerapix.
One of the growing series of *Journey Through...* guides. An excellent souvenir of the country in words and pictures. To read for inspiration before you go or for recalling memories after you get back.

There are a number of novels and adventure stories set in Rhodesia/Zimbabwe and Botswana. The most popular of these are by Wilbur Smith. For an interesting mix of historical fact and romantic fiction buy some of his books before setting out for Southern Africa, or read them while travelling. But note that the fourth book in the Ballantyne series, *The Leopard Hunts in Darkness,* is banned in Zimbabwe.
   Laurence Van Der Post has written a number of books about Botswana including *A Story Like the Wind*, *A Far Off Place*, *The Lost World of the Kalahari*, *The Heart of the Hunter*, and (with Jane Taylor) *Testament to the Bushmen*.
   Zimbabwean writer Geoffrey Ndhala's *The Southern Circle* (Drumbeat/Longmans) is set in Rhodesia before independence, while Doris Lessing's early novel, *The Grass is Singing* evokes the colonial era beautifully, and provides an interesting contrast.

Guidebooks

This book is aimed at independent travellers on a limited budget. There are several other guidebooks which cover all areas of these two countries in more detail.

Zimbabwe, Botswana and Namibia - A Travel Survival Kit (published by Lonely Planet) and *Zimbabwe & Botswana — The Rough Guide* (Rough Guides) both contain good information for independent visitors.

Spectrum Guide to Zimbabwe published by Camerapix.
A mainstream guide, with detailed background information and beautiful photographs.

Visitors Guide to Botswana by Mike Main and John and Sandra Fowkes. Published by Southern Books, Johannesburg (1987). Written primarily for the visitor with a 4WD vehicle, the book has excellent route descriptions on hard-to-get-to places and is recommended for these. Some route descriptions are now very outdated though.

Health manuals
Travellers' Health, Richard Dawood, OUP.
The Tropical Traveller, John Hatt, Pan.

Maps
The Michelin Map of Central and Southern Africa (sheet 155) is widely regarded as the most reliable map of the countries described in this book. It's also useful if you're planning to travel on to South Africa or Zambia, Malawi and Tanzania.

Further Travels in Africa and the Indian Ocean

Guide to Mauritius by Royston Ellis.
A complete guide to every aspect of Mauritius and its dependency, Rodrigues.

Guide to the Comoro Islands by Ian Thorpe.
Four seldom visited islands lying between Madagascar and Africa.

Guide to Madagascar by Hilary Bradt.
How and where to see the island's spectacular wildlife, rainforests and semi-desert. A complete guide for all budgets.

Guide to South Africa by Philip Briggs.
Budget travel and bird-watching, walks and game parks, beaches and cities, suggested itineraries.

Guide to Namibia and Botswana by Chris McIntyre and Simon Atkins.
Off the beaten track in these sparsely populated countries.

Africa Handbooks: Zaire, Malawi, Senegal, Ivory Coast
Four pocket-sized guides to the less-visited countries of Africa.

Through Africa: the overlander's guide by Bob Swain and Paula Snyder.
Driving, motor-cycling, or mountain-biking through the continent. Preparations, routes, campsites, travellers' tales.

Backpacker's Africa — East and Southern by Hilary Bradt.
Hiking and backpacking off the beaten track with an emphasis on natural history. Covers Ethiopia, Eritrea, and Sudan and countries south.

Guide to Zanzibar by David Else.
A detailed guide to the islands of Zanzibar and Pemba.

Guide to Mozambique by Bernhard Skrodzski
The first guide to this former Portuguese colony.

Guide to Tanzania by Philip Briggs
On and off the beaten track in every corner of the country.

Guide to Uganda by Philip Briggs
Includes gorilla viewing in Rwanda and Zaïre.

And then there's the rest of the world...
Send for a catalogue from Bradt Publications, 41 Nortoft Road, Chalfont St Peter, Bucks SL9 0LA, England. Tel/Fax: **0494 873478**.

INDEX

ZIMBABWE

Bulawayo 13-14
Bvumba Mt 49

Cecil Kop Reserve 21
Centenary 46-47
Chimanimani National Park 38-45
Chinhoyi Caves 50
Chipangali Wildlife Orphanage 14

Fort Victoria, *see Masvingo*

Great Zimbabwe (ruins) 19, 52

Harare 14-18
Hwange National Park 51

Inyanga, *see Nyanga*
Inyazura, *see Nyazura*

Kariba 18
Khami (ruins) 14

Lake Kyle Recreation Park 19
Lake McIlwaine Recreation Park 17

Makuti 18
Maleme Dam 26

Mana Pools National Park 51-52
Masvingo 19, 52
Melsetter *see Chimanimani*
Matopos, *see Matobo*
Matobo National Park 14, 24-30
Mavuradonha Wilderness 46-47
Mutare 20, 50

Nyanda, *see Masvingo*
Nyanga National Park 22, 30-38

Salisbury, *see Harare*
Sinoia, *see Chinhoyi*

Tigers Kloof Reserve 21
Tshabalala Sanctuary 14

Umtali, *see Mutare*

Victoria Falls 53-55
Vumba, *see Bvumba*
Vumba Botanical Gardens 49

Wankie, *see Hwange*

Zambezi River 53-55

BOTSWANA

Chobe National Park 66, 76

Francistown 64

Gaborone 63, 65
Ghanzi 64

Kasane 66

Maun 66, 68-73
Moremi Wildlife Reserve 75

Nata 66

Okavango Delta 67-73

Notes

Notes

Notes

Notes

Notes

Notes